W

THE DESIGNING LIFE

W

THE DESIGNING LIFE

by The Staff of W

Edited by Lois Perschetz

*Designed by Justine Strasberg
with Elizabeth Van Itallie*

CLARKSON N. POTTER, INC., PUBLISHERS
DISTRIBUTED BY CROWN PUBLISHERS, INC., NEW YORK

Published by Clarkson N. Potter, Inc., 225 Park Avenue South, New York, New York 10003 and represented in Canada by the Canadian MANDA Group.

CLARKSON N. POTTER, POTTER, and colophon are trademarks of Clarkson N. Potter, Inc.

Manufactured in Japan

Library of Congress Cataloging-in-Publication Data
W, the designing life.
1. Costume designers—Biography.   I. Perschetz, Lois.   II. W.
TT505.A1W2   1986   746.9'2'0922 [B]   86-844
ISBN 0-517-55986-2

10 9 8 7 6 5 4 3 2 1

First Edition

CONTENTS

FOREWORD

I think fashion is like a good meal. You eat it, digest it, and then you go on to something else—like a nice glass of wine. That's the philosophy behind *W*; we look at fashion as it happens, enjoy it—see it as part of the many things that interest us every day. That's why we developed *W* as a full-color newspaper—it's attractive like a magazine but has the speed and immediacy of a daily newspaper.

The secret of *W*, of course, is that we get there first. We're in the workrooms in New York and especially in Europe when the designers are just making their collections, and by that I mean just sewing them up. We show the photographs before the collections are even finished. *W* is really an advance peek at what's going on in the world of fashion.

We also try to present fashion realistically, to put it in its proper perspective. We don't photograph dresses in dramatically lit studios—we take the clothes into homes and restaurants and out onto the streets. I don't consider fashion an art. I never have. I think people who start oohing and aahing over fashion are being pretentious. It does have an important place in our lives in that it's nice to see people looking attractive. I get fed up with people who dismiss fashion and say "Oh, it's the rag trade." When people get up in the morning, they should be able to put on something that makes them look nice and feel good. When I get depressed, I buy a necktie. It makes me feel better.

Fashion is a joy, but it's not to be taken as some great art where everybody drops dead when they see a new dress. That's ridiculous. What they really should drop dead over is the woman who's wearing it; she is much more important than her clothes.

That's why *W* is also about the world of people. *W* started in 1973 and was one of the very first publications to devote a lot of space to people and how they live and enjoy life. We visit world leaders, writers, actors, business giants, film directors, politicians, and especially the designers. People who make things happen.

Does a "designer name" sell fashion? I think it helps. But only if the thing happens to be very attractive, like a beautiful handbag or a piece of jewelry that is really good. Women and men who buy clothes, who buy fashion, aren't stupid. They're very smart. They know what's good. If you lay out fifteen things for an American woman, she will recognize the quality right away and she'll buy the nice thing. I think Americans have the best taste of anybody in the world. (For comfortable houses, though, the English may have the best taste. Fortunately it's interesting that it's all divided. We try to capture that in *W*.)

Just after *W* was started, fashion designers began to become big stars. (The White House, for example, never gives a state dinner without asking a designer.) They're treated as celebrities. They make as much money as rock stars, but unlike the music and movie crowds who generally have absolutely zilch taste, the designers have *great* taste. They know how to do it all: They have the most beautiful homes, they know how to cook better than anybody else, they know how to entertain better than anybody else, and they spend lots of money doing it. Truthfully, I don't know why the designers let us into their homes and their lives. They like it. They appreciate it. I guess they get a reaction when we do it. We get a reaction from it too. Readers like to be involved, to maybe know a little bit more about the style-setters than somebody else does. And to know it first.

More than anyone else, fashion designers set trends—they just do it naturally. That's why it's so much fun to write about them.

—John B. Fairchild

INTRODUCTION

What puts a designer at the head of the pack? A combination of versatility and single-mindedness. An ability to design a complete, diverse collection that embodies a consistently individual point of view.

Each year *W* selects for its pages an international group of designers that is, quite simply, the best. One year there may be twenty-five names toted up, another there may be twenty-seven. For nothing, of course, ever stays the same—especially in the volatile world of fashion. But there is a small group whose names, talent, and influence have staying power. These are the fourteen men and women who comprise the chapters of this book.

Fashion today is the flashiest, most expensive, traveling road show in the world. Designers are powerful personalities. Giant-sized photographs of their faces loom narcissistically out of their own boutiques and on department-store floors in Paris, New York, London, Milan, and Tokyo. They have the glittering charisma and recognition-value of international movie stars. Store appearances turn into media events, and fans besiege designers for autographs everywhere they go. Yet the best creators are much, much more than cosmetic images, to be manipulated by financial gray eminences. The top personalities—Yves Saint Laurent, Bill Blass, and Donna Karan, among others—know their business as well as any B-school graduate.

Moreover, a fashion designer, unlike a creator in the fine arts, is an acknowledged tastemaker. We may be interested to know how a great painter lives or where a prima ballerina parties, but we see how Ralph Lauren decorates his house or Bill Blass cooks his dinner and we may adopt their styles as our own. That is the magic of the designing life.

The articles assembled in this book come, for the most part, from the pages of *W*; a few pieces—such as an interview with up-and-comer Calvin Klein—predate *W*'s 1973 beginnings and were borrowed from *W*'s sister publication, *Women's Wear Daily* (the fashion trade newspaper that is written by the same staff), because they were just too interesting—and too irresistible—to leave out. Many articles are timeless, while others are relevent to the time at which they were written; for that reason, all the pieces carry the dates of when they appeared.

In the pages that follow you will learn about fourteen of fashion's enduring luminaries through interviews, news stories, party coverage, lifestyle pieces, and, of course, the remarkable body of work each generates season after season. You'll see close up how they earn their money—sometimes *lots* of money—and how they spend it. In short, through all the divergent facets, from the sublime to the ridiculous, of their lives as designers.

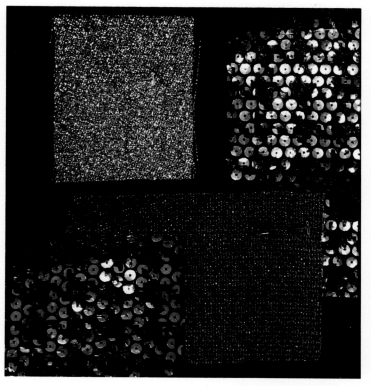

RICH RI

From the mountains of Colorado to the souks of Marrakech, the world's Designing Rich are showing their financial strength. On both sides of the Atlantic a small group of designers has turned fashion into fortune. Although none of them makes his money in pursuits generally associated with great wealth—natural resources, steel, real estate, energy—today's designers make and spend more money than movie stars or corporate executives.

When you earn the kind of money these designers do, they are able to indulge whims, live like Romans, and let others worry about the details. Because of the lucrative nature of licensing these men and women are accumulating personal wealth at a rate almost as dizzying as the speed of their jets.

Ralph Lauren, for example, probably made more than $15 million in 1986. A few others—among them Calvin Klein, Karl Lagerfeld, and Oscar de la Renta—are not far behind.

These are huge amounts of money, even after taxes, and they give rise to lifestyles that range from bizarre to Byzantine. For Ralph Lauren, for example, it means four homes: a sprawling ranch in Colorado, a Manhattan duplex, a beach house in the Hamptons, and a getaway home in Jamaica's Montego Bay. Furthermore, he is said to be building an out-of-the-way showplace in Westchester County, New York. For the proper touch of elegance, Lauren has an English butler.

Here's how the Rich Designers make their money—and how they spend it.

PARIS—French designers have their secrets. A tiny atelier in a shadowy quarter of Paris that makes exquisite costume jewelry, for example. But perhaps their most zealously guarded secret is the size of their own burgeoning wealth. As Karl Lagerfeld, who is easily one of the planet's best-paid dressmakers and probably its most outspoken as well, puts it: "It's not a good idea to let people know how much money you have. It could be dangerous. It is always better to be conservative when talking numbers." Indeed, most of them first throw up a haughty, "I don't know," when asked about their finances. It is only when pressed that someone such as Claude Montana, relatively new to the fortunes an imaginative designer can haul in, will break down and name a figure.

Montana says he makes "around" a million dollars a year, a sum composed of royalties from seven franchised boutiques around the world, licenses in Japan, and his

CH RICH

own salary, coming from the French-based Montana business, whose volume hits about $35 million. "My greatest luxury," he says, "is not having to worry about money."

Montana rents an apartment on the Left Bank but is shopping for a residence in Paris. He recently purchased a summer hideaway in Capri, employs a maid, has a driver for his BMW, and collects modern art. However, he finally whimpers: "I really don't have that much. Seventy-three percent of my income is devoured by taxes."

In contrast, Emanuel Ungaro becomes as reclusive as a hermit when the question of money comes up. However, according to an Ungaro aide, all products bearing his name last year rang up a retail volume of about $600 million (roughly $300 million wholesale). This includes a rapidly growing range of licensed products. Currently his business juggles some 120 licensees worldwide.

But the designer himself, who makes the final decisions in the business he has owned on an equal basis with partner Sonia Knapp for the past twenty-one years, is reportedly on the miserly side with his own salary. For all the hours he toils, and he is known for working long ones, it is estimated he draws only about $500,000 a year. Spartan-like, he drives an Austin Mini, runs around the office turning lights off, and is known to keep his staff at the office until six

o'clock on Christmas Eve. If Ungaro indulges himself, it may be with his perfume, Diva, produced by Chanel. It did $13 million worth of business in 1985, and his 2 percent royalty share means he pocketed $360,000—in his own pocket, it is said, not the company's. Society-shy Ungaro rents an apartment in Paris and owns only one home, in the South of France, where his family is based.

The combined incomes of Yves Saint Laurent and his partner, Pierre Bergé, are said to be closing in on that of Pierre Cardin (who, with an estimated annual income of more than $10 million, is probably Europe's wealthiest designer). Neither will talk dollars, but colleagues estimate Saint Laurent, who owns 60 percent of his business, makes just over $5 million a year. "But that figure has nothing to do with his buying power," confides one. "He could spend twice that tomorrow on anything he likes."

YSL's Rue de Babylon apartment, filled with priceless antiques and paintings by Goya, Matisse, Leger, Munch, Klee, Picasso, and Cézanne, is a monument to his stylish way with a franc. With Bergé, he also owns the opulent Chateau Gabriel in Normandy, a New York apartment, and a sprawling village in Marrakech.

The designer, whose products have an estimated retail turnover of $1,250,000,000, has more than 200 licenses. (The company reportedly gets $1 million alone from R.J. Reynolds, which has the privilege of manufacturing cigarets under the designer's name.) The U.S. is said to generate profits of $14 million and the rest of the world about $30 million. Saint Laurent also receives a small royalty from Charles of the Ritz, which produces the highly profitable perfumes and cosmetics line. But this is considerably less than is generally supposed, since Saint Laurent and Bergé several years ago gave up most of their fragrance rights in exchange for full control of the fashion house, which Charles of the Ritz once owned.

Determining Karl Lagerfeld's income is like counting snowflakes in a blizzard. Besides a rumored personal fortune of considerable size, the designer also has a staggering number of free-lance fashion contracts, some of which the world knows about, and some of which Lagerfeld keeps deftly hidden. Heeding his own advice to be circumspect, Karl Lagerfeld says he stopped counting his money. But his annual income is now said to hover around the $6 million mark, thanks to the fact that, as he says, "I accept no job under $1 million." Most of that income comes from stratospheric straight fees he receives from Fendi in Rome (a fancy apartment of his choosing is also thrown into the deal), Chanel in Paris, and Elizabeth Arden in the United States, which pays him royalties on sales of products manufactured under the Parfums Largerfeld banner. The combined volumes of Chloé (named after the fashion house where he worked for twenty years), KL for Men, and KL for Women fragrances are put at $100 million and Largerfeld splits royalties of between 4 and 5 percent with London-based Dunhill, Chloé's owners. His two signature ready-to-wear collections produced under license by Bidermann Industries in France and in the U.S., on the other hand, "are unimportant in the balance of my personal finances."

As Lagerfeld is the first to point out, unlike many designers, all of the money he earns is private income and, therefore, is saved from the fate of reinvestment in the always precarious apparel business. He has virtually no overhead; most of his assistants are paid by the various clients, and he has no revenue-guzzling fashion house to maintain.

Lagerfeld is no spendthrift, and the first place his money is likely to go is into eighteenth-century furniture and paintings. Three years ago, he paid a mere $450,000 for a famous set of twelve bergeres (large, deep armchairs) and two matching settees. The other day, someone offered him $1,200,000 for the lot. He isn't selling. Lagerfeld has a zillion other stories just like this one in which he comes out the winner, and, for this reason, he says it is impossible to estimate his personal wealth.

For nine years, Lagerfeld has rented (and decorated no less than four times) a spacious apartment in Paris in the Rue de L'Universite. But he is a heavy real estate owner in the playground where he officially resides, Monaco. There, Lagerfeld owns two apartments totaling 850 square meters—real estate that could be worth between $6,400,000 and $9,000,000. Not that he has set up housekeeping in either of these digs. "In Monaco, you don't always live in the place you own," he explains. "That's the secret there." He also has his Chateau de Penhoit, planted on 24 acres near Vannes in Brittany where, he says, "I've turned a nice little castle into a mini-Versailles."

MILAN—Perhaps it's quirk of the Italians, but several of the country's top fashion designers seem not to mind talking about their pay. The accuracy of the numbers may at times be in doubt. Nonetheless, with queries, the figures spin out.

A lot of industry sources say that Valentino is probably the highest-paid designer in Italy. However the Chic's business partner, Giancarlo Giammetti, claims Valentino takes home only around $250,000 a year. That's not a lot for someone sitting on the majority of shares in a company Giametti values at close to $50 million. Valentino enjoys, however, a number of company perks, such as his yacht, the *T. M. Blue*. Now, the designer claims to be seeking a new cruiser, in the $7 million range.

Valentino's skills have also garnered him a sprawling villa on Capri, overlooking the water but fitted with its own swimming pool. The designer also has homes in Gstaad, New York, and Rome, where he is based.

Giorgio Armani says he really doesn't know how much he makes—but he vividly remembers how much he had to pay in 1985 personal income taxes: $640,000. Based, roughly, on Italian tax rates, that puts Armani's income at a minimum of $1,200,000 a year.

Where does the Armani money go? "I have three houses that cost me a lot to keep up," he says. In addition to his home in Milan, he has a house in Forte dei Marmi, about 45 minutes outside of Florence. It's modest, but has a gym and pool. For summer days, there is the ultra-private villa in Pantelleria.

In cars, Armani favors a Mercedes coupe that his late partner, Sergio Galeotti, gave him. He says he'll never give it up. He doesn't collect art because "I'd get too attached to it." He does invest in the stock market, but adds, "I don't even have a broker."

Like many of Milan's newer generation of designers, Gianfranco Ferre plows a lot of potential income back into the firm he co-owns with Franco Mattioli (though Ferre owns the majority). Mattioli claims that Ferre's salary currently is not more than $200,000, because of his desire to put the money back into the business.

Ferre says he doesn't think a lot about what he makes, but he enjoys knowing "I buy what I like." What Ferre likes includes modern art. Among his pearls are two paintings by Picasso and a Modigliani. Besides his main residence in a small town on the outskirts of Milan, Ferre has a villa on Lake Maggiore, for weekends, and a pied à terre in Milan.

NEW YORK—A Grumman Gulfstream jet glides onto the airstrip in Ridgway, Colorado, and expels the diminutive figure of a man clad in well-worn jeans and flannel shirt. An equally seasoned Jeep makes its way with him aboard—through the aspens to a 10,000-acre ranch of the most studiously rustic splendor money can buy. The man is Ralph Lauren, and his after-tax income this year should be about $15 million to $20 million.

Masses of sumptuous Denning & Fourcade scarlets—fringe, silk, tapestry—are in the process of being abandoned by Oscar de la Renta, as he seeks the sleeker comforts of decorator-architect Thierry Des Pont. De la Renta, sources comment, could earn nearly $5 million this year—and can buy all the sleekness he wants.

Calvin Klein, with a net worth some observers ballpark at about $100 million, will probably spend part of it on Southwestern art, his passion. In a different mood, not too long ago, he spent about $70,000 on a black Mercedes 560 SEL.

And as for Bill Blass, he indulges himself with such bibelots as his collection of trompe l'oeil paintings from the seventeenth and eighteenth centuries. Such purchases are made possible by a net worth Blass watchers put at $30 million to $40 million, a level where Oscar too may be ranked—if not higher.

Ralph Lauren, with his richly textured WASP fantasies; Blass, with his soignée charm; Oscar, with his sultry romanticism; and Calvin, with his obsessive sensualism, are old hands in this golden circle, a class of hard-working creators who make lots of dollars and spend them with gusto.

Ralph Lauren is not demure when quizzed about his personal wealth. "I'm going to throw up. I can't talk about it," he said. The $300 million estimate of his total wealth makes him the richest of American designers. It's a fortune he has built from a welter of products—from apparel to fragrance to furniture—that this year are expected to do $625 million wholesale.

Lauren's directly owned company, Polo/Ralph Lauren, produces the designer's expensive men's wear and handles the licensing. Bidermann Industries does his women's lines, and probably the most profitable of his international licensing agreements is with Cosmair, for men's and women's fragrances, which does a worldwide volume of $125 million. There's also a home in Montego Bay, Jamaica. Other elements of the Lauren fantasy include his collection of antique cars, said to be worth $20 million. For everyday driving, he has a $52,000 black Porsche. And there's a storehouse of art and antiques, much of it on display in his Madison Avenue store.

While spinning out visions of the most sensual sort, Calvin Klein has become even more the Seventh Avenue magnate. In 1983, he and his business partner, Barry Schwartz, bought Puritan Fashions Corp., the manufacturer that provided Klein with streams of licensing money for its production of Calvin Klein jeans. When Schwartz and Klein moved to refinance their acquisi-

tion, documents required by the SEC confirmed the designer's staggering earning power. In 1984, Klein earned—including cash dividends and other distributions from his businesses—$12,347,000. Schwartz pulled in the same.

Now that they own Puritan, the licensing percentage isn't as grand as it was, but Klein has developed some other thriving licensees, such as his Obsession fragrance, which undoubtedly keeps earning power up to snuff. Meanwhile, Klein, Schwartz, and crew have been busy turning Puritan around, from a loss of over $11 million in 1984 to profit of over $12 million in 1985. All the products bearing the designer's name could be hitting well over $500 million at wholesale, with Puritan alone contributing $185 million in 1985.

When it comes to spending, Klein prefers a minimalist environment fused with high-tech. His Central Park West duplex apartment in New York, said to be worth some $2,500,000, has wraparound stereo, fancy remote controls, and comes complete with rooftop garden, workout gym—and Georgia O'Keeffe paintings. In a nod to the past, he collects antique watches. He has houses on Fire Island and in Key West.

Oscar de la Renta's name may well mean more than $225 million in wholesale sales this year, and that could mean close to $5 million in income each for de la Renta and his business partner, Gerald Shaw. Their directly owned business puts out two lines—their high-priced, ready-to-wear collection and the more moderate Miss O. line, which together do an estimated volume of less than $20 million. Licensing royalties provide the big payoff and a major contributor is the fragrance line done by Parfums Stern, which reportedly does an annual volume of more than $60 million.

The cash gives the designer the wherewithal to exercise his way with the niceties of life—beautiful flowers and luxurious linens, but his lifestyle is undergoing a change, to go with a change in residence. He recently sold, for a reported $3,500,000, the elegant but traditionally furnished apartment he shared with his late wife, Françoise, and purchased an eight-room co-op on Park Avenue for just over $2 million.

De la Renta also practices the art of hospitality at his Caribbean hideaway, a compound at Casa de Campo, a stylish resort area in the Dominican Republic. He has three houses there: one to live in, one to sleep in, and a guest house. For still another change in scene, the designer has a country place in Kent, Connecticut.

The ever-urbane Bill Blass presides over a fashion empire whose wholesale volume approaches an estimated $150 million. Most of it is brought in by licensed merchandise and could give Blass, by some counts, up to $6 million in income this year.

Putting some of that money to work, Blass recently had his penthouse on 57th Street and Sutton Place—valued at easily $2 million—redecorated by Mica Ertegun and Chessy Rayner.

In addition to the penthouse, Blass has a country home on 22 acres in Preston, Connecticut. The main building is an eighteenth-century structure that once was a tavern. A regular at Christie's, Blass has filled both his New York apartment and his Connecticut stone house with antiques and art.

Around this constellation of golden designers, a host of other fashion stars come and go, some developing their own Midas touch. Formerly a codesigner at Anne Klein, Donna Karan was given her own company by Anne Klein's backers late in 1984, and made an immediate impact. Karan owns 50 percent of the company, but insists it's a "baby company," and that she won't be seeing any profit from it for another two years. Her salary, according to one executive, is "close to seven figures, plus bonus and incentives," but Karan herself says: "I earn more than $500,000, but less than a million."

Karan rents a four-bedroom apartment on Manhattan's Upper East Side. It accommodates several large sculptures by her husband, Stephan Weiss, as well as the antique furniture she collects. She also is buying a house in the Water Island community on Fire Island.

In contrast, Norma Kamali, known for listening to different drummers, is a designer deliberately contracting her business. Earlier this year, her six-year licensing agreement with Jones Apparel Group for Kamali sportswear ended a deal which brought her an average $1,500,000 in royalties yearly. She also pulled out of a fragrance licensing deal in the effort to gain control of her destiny, which includes her second New York store, opened in September, in Soho. Still, Kamali says: "I'm earning more than I ever thought I would. I mean, I thought the most I'd ever make was about $90 a week as a painter."

VALENTIN
The Roman Emperor
of Fashion

Born Valentino Garavani in 1932, he opened a couture house in Rome in 1959, and by the time he reached his early thirties, one name had become enough: Valentino.

Known for his unabashedly glamorous and opulent clothes, Valentino can also portion out subtlety with exquisite control. His fascination with the feminine form began when he was a schoolboy in Voghera, where he sketched dresses in his books. At seventeen, he took off for Paris, working as a sketcher at Jean Desses and then at Guy Laroche before returning to Italy in 1958. A year later he started his couture house, where he was joined in 1960 by Giancarlo Giammetti, his partner since. Though he shows his ready-to-wear in Paris, where his couture equals are, Valentino continues to bring his own couture coterie to Rome.

The impresario of a far-reaching fashion empire that includes fifty-eight licensees throughout the world, Val also dresses men and children, and gives women everything from swimsuits to skiwear. He is a man who prides himself on professionalism and precision, signaled by his impeccable grooming and eternal tan. Says Giammetti, "He's the world's biggest dreamer," his sensibility indulged in a lifestyle so splendid it seems to be from another era—a lifestyle that includes four fabulous homes and a yacht, and that, in the same spirit as his clothes, has earned him the sobriquet, "the Chic."

THE VALENTINO

The tortoiseshell cigaret holder never far from his pursed lips tells it all: extravagant, ferociously chic, a trifle flashy, glamorous "to die" (as he might put it), confident, vain, and above all, hazardous to your health, at least financially.

It's a rich sauce that Valentino brews, both in his clothes and in his way of life, and it's not to everyone's taste. But no one can deny that the Valentino style possesses flair, originality, and springs from a recipe only the ripest Romans know about. "I have the privilege of age, the privilege to be secure," the designer asserts. "And I'm very, very secure."

He's also wealthy, the linchpin of a fashion empire that does $300 million a year in business.

And Valentino does spend it. There's a mountainside chalet in Gstaad for the winter, a luxurious yacht for summer cruises, a Moorish palace on Capri for weekends, and a new apartment in New York for the odd dinner. To rest after work, there's a twenty-eight-room villa on the Appian Way, complete with a man-made pond and scores of white-gloved servants.

When he moves, he moves like a head of state, his chauffeured Mercedes sandwiched between two Fiats full of brawny bodyguards. "I hate all that, I really do," insists Valentino. "I'd much rather take a taxi, like the Prime Minister's wife, but they tell me I can't."

The Roman mansion is also heavily guarded, to protect Valentino and to safeguard the treasures within. He spends most evenings alone there, closeted behind the dozen doors leading to his private apartment. Weekends, whether spent at another of his homes or on his yacht, are usually more gregarious, though not any less luxurious.

On Sunday nights Valentino is back in Rome, for he is a man who is serious about his profession and is very quick to point out that all is not glamorous. "I am a worker by nature and at heart. It is what I like best.

"All the time, they are criticizing, clutching at you . . . they need your merchandise, they need your beautiful things. Everything happens at once during the day. We jump, thirty minutes to an hour, from one thing to another. You cannot imagine the problems that develop when I go away for a short four-day vacation. Always with couture and ready-to-wear collections, men's wear, home furnishings, and all the other license programs, a designer's life is not soft. In the end, the responsibility is mine. Yes, of course, there are the couture shows and the parties afterward, dinners and lunches at wonderful restaurants—but I am happiest when my work is going well."

And, he says, "If you want to do well, you have to work a lot, and I want to control everything in my business."

Although Valentino generally defers to his business partner, Giancarlo Giammetti, for specifics about his operation, it is clear that the designer knows precisely what is going on and can tell you, to the lira, the number of orders he received for his last couture collection. "I am very conscious, more and more, to feel the acceptance of a collection—how well it's sold," he admits frankly. "I am not the kind of designer to create a collection that the papers talk about, but never sells. When you do a collection, you are pushed to do something extravagant for the sake of the show; in fact, there are people who have a collection backstage for the buyers. That's not right.

"Believe me, it's very hard when you have to sell the collection and it's so extravagant. You cannot sell stupid, crazy things with high prices. Leave that to the smaller designers with cheap prices. Creativity and ideas in details and shapes are needed, but designs always must be wearable."

In his search for perfection, Valentino works long hours in his studio, finally leaving at about eight or nine at night, and has been known to throw out $60,000 worth of costume jewelry the night before a couture collection because "it didn't look quite right."

Actions such as that take confidence, and, at fifty-one, the tanned, impeccably groomed Valentino seems to have come into his own. In his fashion, the fussy flourishes and ruffles of earlier collections have been tossed aside, like the costume jewelry. In their place is a new restraint, sleek and elegant female clothes, still very strong on luxury, but infinitely more sophisticated and subtle.

The right way to live, according to the Valentino creed, is to be surrounded by beautiful objects and dressed in a fashion that is pleasing to the eye. "I was born like that, wanting to dress nicely and to see beauty all around me," he adds. "I love beautiful houses filled with beautiful furniture and beautiful objects. I love to see a beautiful table and to change china and the colors in a house.

"Life is very difficult. We have lots of problems today. We are all a little nervous, a little hysterical. Not me. I am calm. I pretend a lot—perfection, professionality, a good education, and lots of experience."

Although he dresses everyone from Jackie O ("I owe a big percentage of my fame to her") to Marie-Hélène de Rothschild, Valentino is hard put to credit the inspiration for his designs. "There are no more muses for me," he says, sadly shaking his head. "I am proud when these ladies wear my clothes, but today when I dream about somebody, I look to my models and try to create a mirror for my ladies. Besides, the ladies today are so fickle. They wear a Saint Laurent blouse with an Ungaro skirt and somebody else's shoes."

But he's still mad for those ladies and loves to surround himself with the grand names of this world whenever the opportunity arises. And they love to be with him, not least of all because Valentino doesn't stint. When he gives a lunch at Le Cirque, he prints his own menus and gives the chef the recipes. And when he throws a party for himself, the tab can reach upwards of half a million dollars.

Nowadays, he seems happiest in Gstaad, the ghetto resort for millionaires, where he can practice his downhill racing. "When I look out and see the perfect white snow without a footprint, I think that is the most wonderful place to be," he says. "And when I am there, I think, now I will just work on my style."

—ROME, 1984

STYLE

"Very chic women like to wear things for a long time—to me, this is the key of chic. An evening gown will last two, maybe three seasons, providing you have other dresses to alternate with, but suits and coats can go on for years."

Fitting a couture collection, 1982

Valentino's Villa: Simply Opulent

Although Valentino refers to his mansion on the Appian Way as "my typical Roman villa," there is nothing mundane about this twenty-eight-room extravaganza.

If anything, the house, which Valentino recently redecorated with the help of Milanese architect Renzo Mongiardino, is the fusion of two great personal fantasies: Mongiardino's passion for the gilded salons of the late nineteenth century and Valentino's penchant for unabashed opulence.

But Valentino denies all such pretensions. "I wanted something cozy and comfortable," he says, "a place where I could casually entertain my friends and where I could show off the objects I've collected over a lifetime." And they are all here—the Ming statues and the Miró sketches, the chubby-figured Boteros and the sable-draped chairs around Valentino's gargantuan neoclassic bed, the nineteenth-century black marble candelabra and the ripped Fontana canvases, the sharp ivory tusks and the gold faucets, the space-age video equipment and the private snapshots of Callas, Baryshnikov, and, of course, Jackie O.

Only the flamingos that used to frolic in front of the house are gone. They succumbed to the Roman summer heat and the exhaust fumes from the commuter traffic just beyond the estate's acre-long lawn and high stone wall.

Valentino bought the villa, a few steps from the Catacombs, in 1969 and estimates that it was built in the Twenties. Last April Valentino decided it was time to shake up his life. "I was getting bored," he explains. "It's my belief that every house should be changed dramati-

Clockwise from top left: The house on the Appian Way; the downstairs video salon; a table with blue marble figurines in the main salon; the entrance hall and main staircase

Valentino's bedroom

The adjoining study and bathroom

The main salon with several clusters of sofas and tables

The fireplace in the main salon

The table set for lunch on the veranda overlooking the pool

cally every five or six years. It may be expensive, but it's absolutely necessary." So he called in Mongiardino, probably the most respected interior designer in Italy, and the two set out to create a mix of what Valentino calls "England and China plus a few places in between."

The work took nine months and was unveiled at a dinner party Valentino gave after his couture show. While a jeans-clad Gianni Agnelli flirted with blonde mannequins and "Superman" Christopher Reeve flexed his muscles, the couturier led his guests about the colorful maze, his platoon of black pugs trailing him.

His favorite room is the upstairs den, with its bright green marble fireplace, its red velvet chairs, and its Fernando Botero portraits, from which Valentino and Mongiardino took the colors for the room's flower-painted-silk walls.

The den is full of real flowers as well, and even when he is at another house or on his yacht, Valentino has the Chinese vases kept filled with pink apple blossoms. "It's an obvious extravagance," he notes, "but I like the thought that even when I'm not here, the house is alive."

Valentino says that he and Mongiardino "worked together like a team." He claims there were few arguments and that the decorator, who created most of the ceramic walls, the elaborate upholstery, and the curtains in his own ateliers, always deferred to his final judgment.

The team's most impressive achievement is the long main salon next to the den, which is as big as most New York apartments. The columned walls are stark white, but the clusters of chairs and couches are covered in pleasing flower-printed chintzes. The round wooden tables are crammed with Oriental objects, and corners are hidden with gigantic potted plants and lacquer screens. It is a sumptuous mélange, dominated, as Valentino and Mongiardino intended, by the white stone fireplace.

The room is festooned with sparkling ancient swords and Chinese temple statues, which almost, but not quite, overshadow Valentino's impressive collection of modern European art. "I wanted everything I love in this room," explains Valentino. —ROME, 1982

A corner of the main salon with a Picasso

Sailing Chic

Valentino's sexy *T. M. Blue*

Shoes off

Every Friday night of the summer, at 7:30 exactly, Valentino, his favorite pug, Oliver, and a few friends pile into a limousine and drive to a yacht basin an hour north of Rome. There they climb aboard the designer's eighty-five-foot yacht, have a dinner prepared by the chief engineer, and then contentedly sail away. "The boat means peace," sighs Valentino. "I hate to get off."

And who wouldn't? With four luxurious berths, each with its own shower, bath, and telephone; a video system worthy of a Bel-Air mansion; a captain and a five-man crew; a butler; two massive teakwood decks, and fuel capacity to sail two hundred hours, coming home—even for someone with four homes on land—must be heartbreakingly difficult. The boat is called *T.M. Blue,* a name derived from the first initials of Valentino's parents and the yacht's color. The designer had it built to his precise specifications at the Benetti

Lunching on the deck: The Chic with Doris Brynner (*aft*), Georgina Brandolini, and Carlos de Sousa

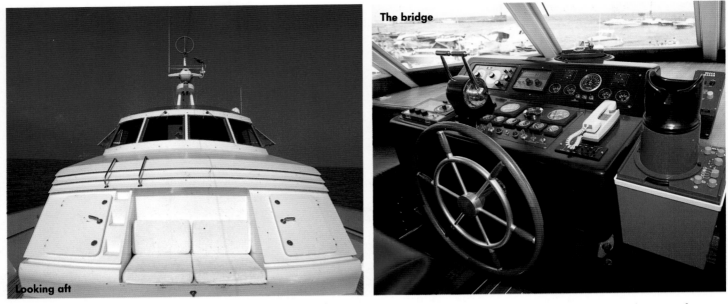

The bridge

Looking aft

Shipyards, considered one of the best in the world, and he decorated the interior himself. Although Valentino is known for the sumptuous settings of his houses, he prefers simplicity—or at least his idea of simplicity—for the yacht. "Boats mean wicker and straw and cotton awning," he says. "I hate the idea of a fancy boat. Velvet and carpets and all that belong on the Avenue Foch, not on the sea."

Still, the *T.M. Blue* isn't Spartan by anyone's standards. The paneling is mahogany, the fittings are brass, and the galley is as modern as you can get. And the food, which is seaman simple, is extraordinarily good. Usually it's salads, fresh fried fish, and delicious Neapolitan ice cream. "Never anything heavy," insists the designer, who is tickled by the notion that while preparing hors d'oeuvres his chef must periodically dash to the bridge to make sure the engine is chugging along correctly.

Usually Valentino takes short cruises to Capri and the smaller islands near it, but this month he's going to Corsica and the South of France. After that, the yacht goes back to Benetti for cosmetic surgery. "We need another bedroom," explains Valentino rather nonchalantly, "so I'm having it added on."
—CAPRI, 1982

Carlos and Georgina going overboard

Outdoor living spaces

Splashy Splendor in Capri

The pool, outfitted with a canopy

ew live on Capri in the grand manner of Valentino. When he arrives by yacht for the weekend, he retires to the luxury of his bougainvillaea-swathed Villa Cercola, an expensive 100-year-old mansion. "Besides Sardinia, where can you go?" he asks, knowing it could only be here.

—CAPRI, 1984

A mass of outdoor color

The cool white interior

THE CHIC AT PLAY

Giorgia Sant'Angelo with Marina Schiano

Giancarlo Giammetti

Send In The Clowns

"It's Italy in exile, with enough props and costumes to make two Fellini movies," mused Lester Persky in the middle of the all-night madness that was Valentino's birthday party, staged in Studio 54 with circus costumes that were, in fact, designed by Fellini for his movie *The Clowns.*

Special guests arrived around midnight through the back entrance into a chiffon-draped area behind a curtain, where they were greeted by clowns with trumpets, dwarfs dressed as clowns, a  man with a monkey on his shoulder, and two makeup girls who latched on to various guests to paint Emmet Kelly faces on them. Finally, sparklers were lit and the curtain rose, spilling the swelling crowds into the disco dressed in masks, elaborate feather headgear, and other plumage.

"I wanted a circus, only more decadent," said party host Giancarlo Giammetti, who had pulled the party together in just two days. "We're living in such a depressing way in Italy that perhaps we need a little extravagance."

The curious mix of people ran the gamut from Gianni Uzielli, very much the observer in his conservative suit, to high-strutting, muscle-rippling Mr. Universe. Egon Von Furstenberg thought Valentino was appropriately dressed as ringmaster: "That's the way he runs his business; he's the boss."

Valentino held court and surveyed the scene with his usual composure, finally leaving the still-raging party at 4 A.M. "Everybody was busy doing their own thing, so I went home," he said with a shrug.   —NEW YORK, 1978

The Ringmaster and Fellini-costumed friends

Lynn Wyatt and
Giancarlo Giammetti

Raquel Welch

Babbling Brooke Shields
and the Chic

Christmas tree ornaments Doris
Brynner and Georgina Brandolini
decorate Baryshnikov

Veronica and Muhammad Ali;
Norris Church and Norman Mailer

Marisa Berenson

A few Valentinos

Night of the Chic

After a summer devoted principally to crucial if excruciating cosmetic touch-ups, I, Louise J. Esterhazy, return to Manhattan to find myself at the center of a social maelstrom that could cause my newly rejuvenated face to age all over again. That ringmaster of the extravagant, the Chic of Rome, Valentino, held a perfectly elegant gala at the Metropolitan Museum for nearly a thousand of his closest friends, and if I felt exhausted by the end, Valentino must have felt like a pepless peplum.

No skinflint Val—his scale of entertaining is commensurate with the prices he charges his grand-entrance-loving couture customers—the ticket for the whole evening was estimated at $700,000, according to aide-de-Chic Giancarlo Giammetti.

"I don't know, I don't want to know," said spaniel-eyed G, with a solid two hours of sleep behind him, when I gently asked him to break down the costs of the event the next morning. "If you start to ask how much it costs, you can't afford it." Add up the following little expenses: a staff of 80 highly ornamental men from Glorious Foods; 13 European journalists flown over and

boarded courtesy of the Chic just for the gala; 38 models for a full-scale showing of Valentino's fall couture collection, staged in the Pool Room by Michael Arcenaux; and dinner from GF for an intime 325.

For dinner, there was feuilleté d'homard to start, with a La Foret Macon Villages, 1980, to wash it down; fillet of beef au foie gras with green beans and julienne potatoes, accompanied by a nice château Beycheville St. Julien, 1976; and to finish, figs and raspberries with slimming crème fraîche, with Perrier-Jouët Brut. And the trappings from the Great Hall to the Temple of Dendur, where the dinner was held, were appropriate to the worship of the Saint of Chicliness. There were 1,500 votive candles, laced with gardenias, alongside and in the temple's pool, where palm fronds floated, recalling the days of the Chic's ancestress, Cleopatra. And the sang-de-boeuf dinner plates actually had been brought by fastidious Val to make the table setting perfecto, as we say in dear Roma.

Fun-loving Pat Buckley, who danced later than anyone, lost her favorite Walker early in the evening. "Never

mind," said Popular Pat. "If he wants me, he'll shriek." I did feel that Doris Brynner and Georgina Brandolini—in their ruffled, ruffled, and ruffled Val dresses—would be attractive as Christmas tree ornaments. Politically minded Marina Schiano—who was begged by both Val and Cal (Klein) to wear their dresses that evening—solved the touchy issue by donning black velvet Herrera. Carolina was thrilled.

Balletomane Val must have been in paradiso, what with elfin Mikhail Baryshnikov introducing the fashion show and then sensually eating string beans with his fingers, a mannerism adopted by Babbling Brooke Shields.

I had heard rumors that Val might not be showing his next couture collection in Rome, but GG assures me he will—perhaps, however, not at the time the other Italian couturiers do. "After all, they come to see Valentino," said modest GG, "so they'll come at any time."—LOUISE J. ESTERHAZY, New York, 1982

VALENTINO 25

1984

1985

1984

1986

"There's plenty of money around, believe me. The big customers are the Italians for the couture; the Americans still spend, and the Arabian people buy big quantities. The French buy only a few things for a season; they know what they need."

1984

1986

1984

1986

1980

1984

1985

1984

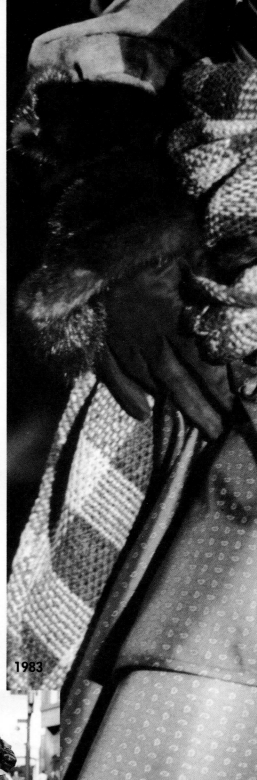

1983

1980

1985

1985

1986

1983

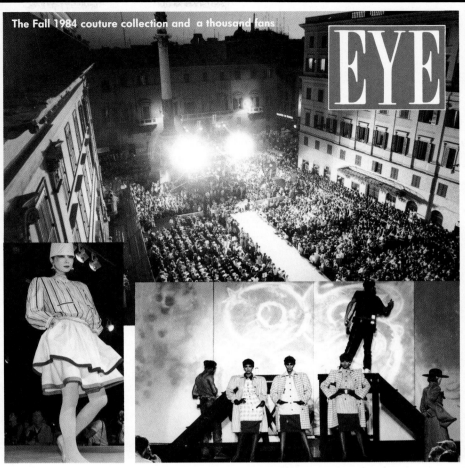

The Fall 1984 couture collection and a thousand fans

HAPPY ANNIVERSARY

It was, after all, Valentino's 50th couture collection, and so it seemed altogether appropriate that the occasion be marked with a regally scaled event that Nero, as they say, would have killed for.

By late evening, while a red Roman sun drenched the city, the Piazza d'Espagna had been covered with 1,000 square meters of black carpet, a 100-foot silver stage glistened in the twilight, and the hordes descended. There was a la dolce vita contingent of Roman socialites in a heavily perfumed haze of sequins, décolletage, and blond hair; smatterings of American actors, Italian rock stars, and politicians; eighty security men (not including private bodyguards); the paparazzi, from a nation who gave us the word; and the thousand or so gente popolare who pressed against the wooden barricades to wonder at it all.

Valentino celebrated as only Valentino would dare, with an epic production that included billowing smoke and a climactic shower of pearls flung over the audience by the models to the strains of "New York, New York."

"When you go on the street with thousands of people watching, you have to give them everything that's Valentino," says Giancarlo Giammetti, the Chic's business partner. "That's not just a show in a room, but something more—well, grand."

Grand indeed. Conveniently located just an elevator ride down from the main floor of Valentino's Via Gregoriana headquarters, the Piazza d'Espagna was taken over for two days, which meant, among other things, clearing the area of cars and recompensing the tiny restaurant behind the Spanish Steps for loss of patronage.

Tickets were distributed at the last minute to avoid establishing a black market in invitations, which reportedly went up to two million lire last year.
—ROME, 1984

"This is my favorite of all my homes," says Valentino of his chalet in Gstaad. "It is here that I forget everything. Work, all the problems and crises in Europe, they are nonexistent. Living in Italy is not easy these days. One can't escape the enormous situation affecting life, be you rich or poor.

"The chalet gives me serenity, calmness. And more important, this is the only house where I can resolve important work problems, although, I never create outside my studio and couture house. I need my office, the fabrics, all the confusion around me."

Gstaad is full of showy chalets, all built with gingerbread-trimmed storybook façades. Valentino's Gifferhorn, named after the mountain the house faces, is one of the most luxe chalets, but it's spacious, modern, and cozy, with no ostentation. Valentino designed the five bedrooms, large living room (with reading and game corner), dining room that seats fourteen, laundry room, garage, two servants' quarters, and kitchen. Swiss architect Matti is responsible for the overall design of the house.

"Matti is the best for designing chalets. He is the one who selects all the exterior and interior woods so essential to the look of mountain chalets," says Valentino. One of the unique features is the façade, which faces Gifferhorn. Long terraces on two upper levels look

out onto the view, which is impressive winter and summer. The large living room is flooded with sunlight that comes through the huge window, but there are large terrace doors that can be left open on a beautiful day to let fresh mountain sun and air blend with the lush scent of Valentino's azaleas.

In fact, the house is always full of the greenest ferns, azaleas, and the scent of rose floris from Cherchez in New York. Mixed with the enduring smells of the best aged and treated woods on the walls and ceiling, these scents give Gifferhorn the exotic aroma of an Oriental palace.

One of the aspects that Valentino likes the most is the Gstaad tradition in architectural design. "Unlike St. Moritz, Gstaad forbids anyone to build a chalet with the look of a modern Monte Carlo villa. The overall look of Gstaad is one of incredible beauty. I think it is one of the most beautiful spots in the world."

The interior of Gifferhorn, however, is quite unlike those of its neighbors. "Most people put velvet curtains and too much richness in Swiss chalets. I wanted a clean, clear, but warm and friendly house," says Valentino.

Most of the cotton fabrics used for everything from the master bedroom's pine-green and off-white dotted walls to the quilted curtains in nearly every room are exclusive prints made for Valentino by the prestigious Paris fabric house Le Manach. Antiques are appropriate and chosen with great care. "Throughout Switzerland there are fine antiques shops. But it is often a long time before you find one with authentic and rare chalet furniture. My sixteenth-century Swiss beds were found near Bern. The first I found by chance, the second I asked a dealer to look for. The best dealers go way up in the mountains for such things as the seventeenth-century Swiss cupboards in the foyer and living room."

The first-level porch of Valentino's chalet, which faces the Gifferhorn Mountain

Life in Gstaad, he says, is centered around the chalet and the ski slopes. "At Gstaad there is a certain warm atmosphere. I used to think I was an ocean person, but I am beginning to like the coziness of life in the snow. Conversations are more animated and intimate. We do not go through all the business of formal sit-down dinners and dressing up. I used to go to St. Moritz from time to time, but I never really liked it. The biggest event of the day turned out to be getting invitations to various dinner par-

"What I like most of all is the relaxed feeling of Gstaad," says Valentino. "Here I feel as if I am always on vacation."

The views, says Valentino, are "incredible"

The Homing Instinct in Gstaad

ties. Then there was the tragedy of one of our guests not getting invited to a party everyone else was. What drama. I cannot support spending a vacation worrying about who is wearing what to whose dinner party. One doesn't have to dress; people are not fashion-conscious." (His friend Doris Brynner, however, recently spent two days in the Palace Hotel selling Valentino couture to ladies who bought dresses for up to $6,000.) Guests, who often make the two-hour drive from the Geneva airport in chauffeured cars or hired taxis that cost "another fortune," include his friends Georgina Brandolini, Alexis de Rede, and Marie-Hélène de Rothschild, who comes with her own maid and personal chauffeur.

A typical day at Gifferhorn: breakfast in bed or gatherings in the breakfast nook before skiing down Wassengrat from the snobbish Eagle Club; tea at the Palace Hotel or a quick sauna or swim; late-afternoon naps; quiet dinners, in sweaters and corduroy jeans.

—GSTAAD, 1978

Norma Kamali is the prime paradox of New York fashion—a shy, self-effacing introvert who wears, and designs, flashy, amusing, and very conspicuous clothes. She also manages to run a business with a tough-mindedness that no one has ever associated with shrinking violets.

The clothes Kamali designs and sells have always made waves. She pioneered HotPants, sweatshirt dressing, big shoulders, "sleeping bag" coats, and swimsuits and dresses at their most revealing. With two collections for Jones Apparel Group and a made-to-order collection sold only at OMO, her shop in New York, Kamali dresses everyone from schoolgirls and secretaries to actresses and rock stars.

Nowhere do her clothes receive more spectacular showcases than in OMO's windows both in the elaborate displays she has devised there and now in the feature fashion videos that play there continually. Kamali feels they are important because they have a stimulating effect upon the store and the immediate neighborhood.

"They're a stage to create anything I want," says Kamali. "I know I have a lot of theater in my soul, and this is a good way to take care of it. Even as a kid, I was shy, but I loved to dress up. So now I dress up other people. They look great, I feel good, and I know my dress went out somewhere special."

NORMA KAMALI
The Flashy Recluse

1985

OSCAR

NORMA KAMALI
The Flashy Recluse

"[Norma Kamali is] just like Edith Bunker—as straight as the day is long. People think she must be some kind of wacko, but she really is the straightest person in the world, just with the most outrageous clothes."

ALL DRESSED UP WITH

1983

When Norma Kamali talks about her childhood, she describes two distinct personalities. She was, on the one hand, the "very shy" little girl, who she remembers was "always drawing alone quietly in the corner." She also was the ponytailed sixth-grader whose classroom wardrobe consisted of eight skirts worn simultaneously, one on top of another—pressed and starched to stick out as far as possible—an angora sweater, and white bucks, which she would touch up with dustings of powder so they'd be white at all times. When she got to class, she had to walk sideways because her skirts wouldn't fit between the rows of desks, and she left a trail of little white footprints wherever she went.

The contradiction inherent in these images is one the designer continues to live out. She remains a reticent, surprisingly plain-spoken woman who happens to design and wear the most imaginative clothes in New York. The spotlight of her immense success glares upon a rather discomfited Kamali. Wearing conspicuously oversized shoulder pads, she gives an interview very grudgingly—citing a host of objections to the idea of designer as cult figure ("I mean, I just dress people")—and responds to a camera aimed at her by reflexively shielding her eyes, like a mole exposed to bright light. She returns from a recent on-foot shopping expedition through Manhattan disconcerted that people recognized her. "This is not good," she says in her deadpan New York drawl. "I can see more when nobody knows who I am."

Kamali is helping to ensure her anonymity by teaching the rest of the world to dress as she does. Longtime couturier to rock and film celebrities with a penchant for unorthodox flash, Kamali struck pay dirt in 1981 when she came out with a line of sweatshirt clothes under the aegis of the Jones Apparel Group, which translated her distinctively shaped broad-shouldered silhouettes at a very affordable price range. The look triggered a small-scale fashion revolution. Suddenly, city streets across America were blanketed with Kamali's

gray, black, and plaid sweat clothes, taking in a weighty $9 million to $10 million for their first year.

Not that Kamali's clothes had negligible visibility before. OMO, her New York boutique, gave birth to the status "sleeping bag" coat, the first in fashion down outerwear; brightly colored suedes, long before the trend swept Seventh Avenue; the most directional, innovative swimwear in the U.S.; and glittering vampish evening clothes.

"She was a quiet influence on international fashion even before the sweats explosion," says Kal Ruttenstein, Bloomingdale's vice-president of fashion direction. "She certainly has the respect of the European designers; they're always interested to know what she's doing. With the sweats, she proved advanced fashion can sell to mainstream America, if it's great value."

Kamali's world took shape in a predominantly Catholic neighborhood on Manhattan's Upper East Side near John Jay Park, where Kamali—born Norma

Kamali in her New York boutique

Arraez in 1946, of Basque-Lebanese descent—grew up. Her childhood and adolescence, as she describes them, have the all-American resonance of an *Archie* comic book in an urban environment.

"We had a great neighborhood," says Kamali, evocatively chewing a stick of gum with real Fifties verve. "The kids

1985

NO PLACE TO HIDE

were the most gorgeous children. When I look back at the pictures, I say it's not true, the kids are so pretty. My father ran the ice-cream parlor—I'm talking serious candy store. My mother, a housewife, was a very creative woman. There was this settlement house where we all went and put on plays with the kids from the neighborhood—you know, little song-and-dance things, like 'Our Gang' comedies. Well, my mother made the most incredible costumes; I mean, she'd do serious research."

Kamali's mother made most of her daughter's everyday clothes as well. "She was an obvious influence. She could make things out of almost anything—you know, dollhouse furniture made out of kitchen things, dish-towel dolls, paper flowers, anything and everything."

The esthetic sense instilled by her mother was broadened when she became old enough to roam Manhattan. "I was very fortunate growing up in the city." She remembers spending lots of time in museums and, by early adolescence, in department stores, especially around Christmas. "I'd parade to each store," she recalls. "I had the sense that I was little and looking at something very grand. I'd love the displays, the old wood counters, the glass. And Bendel's—oh my God, Henri Bendel, with the Rolls-Royces pulling up every three seconds. There was a feeling and an energy that I loved. I'd watch and watch and try not to be seen."

Throughout this period, Kamali spent a lot of time drawing (she hoped to become an artist) and experimenting with creative dressing, including her short-lived eight-skirted look. "That was the period when I was trying to decide whether to be a rocker on the streets or a decent human being. But I couldn't deal with being bad; that was not my experience."

Still, she wasn't exactly the conventional teenager of the times. She remembers dressing for the Peppermint Lounge, her favorite nightly hangout: "When I went out dancing my hair reached heights previously unknown, and I used to stitch myself into my pants because I wanted them right on the body. I also started using shoulder pads. I have little shoulders, and I wanted them to look big. I was always doing strange things."

Acknowledging that being a painter was "a very expensive career," Kamali

decided to become a fashion illustrator. She graduated from the Fashion Institute of Technology, but she felt her best training came from the anatomy classes she took on her own time. In 1964 she took an office job with Northwest Orient airlines, and used the opportunity to spend virtually every weekend from 1964 to 1968 in London. "I'd sleep on the plane going over, and I wouldn't sleep again until I was on the plane going

1983

home. I've never seen anything like the energy in London at that time."

It was the era of King's Road and Carnaby Street. Kamali remembers staying out all night at clubs and parties, where the Rolling Stones, the Beatles, and Jimi Hendrix were part of the sybaritic landscape. She also recalls, with a particular fondness, the archetypal Sixties boutique, Biba, "the most incredible store I've ever seen, with this marvelous look and atmosphere and tons of energy. Then they got carried away and spoiled something wonderful; it became a department store.

"Everybody had a positive attitude," says Kamali, summing up the Sixties. "Maybe it was all a little too fantasy, too dreamy, but dreams are important. People were experimenting in every way; they weren't afraid to try anything. Some wonderful changes happened to all of us as a result. It was the most creative time I've ever seen. That time of experiment is responsible for

what I'm doing today. I said, 'I'm gonna open up a shop. I know what clothes I want. I know I can do it.'"

And so, of course, she did. In 1968 she and her husband of one year, Eddie Kamali, a Persian student, opened a boutique on East 53rd Street in a tiny basement shop they rented for $285 a month. There, she introduced the first HotPants to New York and began designing in the decorative tradition of Carnaby funk. In 1974 the Kamalis moved to a larger space, this time on the second floor at 787 Madison Avenue.

By then, the new designer had attracted the patronage of the glitter celebrities and BP, and Kamali found her talents expanding onto more sophisticated levels. "I changed completely. Enough of this funk, I said. I started doing suits, lace dresses, delicate things that really are a side of me, too."

She also observed a new spirit of independence in the women who shopped in her store. "They were coming in less and less with their husbands or boyfriends and making their own decisions. Then I started to realize I was growing up too, maturing as a person and as a woman. Women of my generation tended to think a man would always take care of them. That's a terrible responsibility to put on anyone. It's hard enough to take care of yourself."

By 1977 Kamali had divorced her husband and left the boutique they had started together. "I was scared, panicked. I knew I had to start something else right away, but I didn't know if I could do it, if anybody knew who I was, if I could get a sewing machine." Kamali borrowed money "from every friend, every relative, everywhere," and in July 1978, at 6 West 56th Street, she opened her minimally furnished boutique of maximally designed clothes. Its name—OMO, for On My Own—was a banner of Kamali's new independence.

The business, and Kamali herself, thrived. The space was expanded, and her staff grew to thirty-three employees. In the middle of it all sits Kamali, looking like the sorority leader, her 5-foot-4¾-inch frame practically hidden under some combination of her sweats, her hair in two neat schoolgirl braids. Her employees use the metaphor of "extended family" in describing the staff's working relationship, an image with which Kamali agrees. "If something good happens to anyone there's so much joy," she says. "But if somebody wants to hurt us, they learn they don't mess with us." When the alarm bell from the shop sounds in the second-floor offices—signaling the entrance of a suspicious-looking person—all the women on the floor grab scissors and seam rippers and head downstairs.

Says OMO vice-president Liz Bureau, "She works with so much love and passion, it's almost not work. You never hear a bad word about Norma here, never. When people ask us what she's like, we say she's just like Edith Bunker—as straight as the day is long. People think she must be some kind of wacko, but she really is the straightest person in the world, just with the most outrageous clothes."

Correspondingly, people who expect Kamali to be a cloud-gathering esthete are surprised to find her an efficient and demanding businesswoman. "I'm a stable person," says Kamali. "I know what I want and what has to be done to get it. Actually, learning the business part has helped me as a designer tremendously. You can't just have a dream; you've got to learn to make it work."

Success, for Kamali, has brought the proverbial mixture of blessings and curses. She likes the fact it enables her simply to design more and that when other designers copy her, "at least now people know where it's coming from." But while she says she's not the sort of person to be changed radically by it, she doesn't like the effect it has on other people. "I think the designer's role is inflated anyway," she says. "I think it's very exciting when you design clothes and affect people's lives. That's all it should be, though. You don't have to know about the person behind the clothes. The other day Eileen Brennan was wearing one of my tops on the Merv Griffin show, and he asked her what she was wearing. She said, 'Don't you know? They're called Kamalis.' Just like that, like they were a box of Wheaties. I felt very comfortable with that."

Kamali describes herself as "a passionate person and an extremist." Between the ages of sixteen and twenty-six, she says, she went out almost every night. "Sleeping wasn't important. I was afraid I'd miss something." Now she is an equally dedicated Calvinist, and she finds work is always, more or less, with her. She spends most of her waking hours at OMO, almost never taking a day off.

"Almost everything is subsumed into my work. I really do love what I'm doing. I know I'm lucky, and I'm afraid to give it up for a minute. It all depends on how much you want to do it—that's the difference between me and everyone else."   —NEW YORK, 1982

NORMA'S VIDEO VISION

The designer with Carly Simon

Walk by a TV screen on 56th Street this summer and you're likely to see a woman dressed in houndstooth and fake leopard skin nervously fingering her pearls as she confides things to her psychiatrist. A few minutes later, she's sitting down to a Thanksgiving dinner with a family that looks as if it had just left the "Twilight Zone."

Is it vintage Woody Allen or "The Mary Tyler Moore Show" sprung back to life from syndication heaven? Well, if there are gold flags flying outside the windows, you're standing outside the OMO boutique, watching Norma Kamali's fashion video *Interview* to the sounds of Carly Simon's *Spoiled Girl*.

Actually, fashion video is not quite an accurate description, since the designer has directed a thirty-minute film that is part movie, part TV sitcom, part fashion video, and more than one or two parts stream-of-consciousness autobiography. "It's a little film that shows what's going on with women today," says Kamali, who wrote the script. "It was important to establish what she is like—her emotions—which is different from a fashion video, which only deals with the externals of clothes."

It took two days to film, two days to edit, and $100,000 to produce, but Kamali still needed music to accompany it. Unhappy with selections she had heard from some record companies, she called friend and customer Carly Simon to find out if she could listen to the singer's upcoming album. "I walked into the store the next day, all wrapped up in my Walkman, screaming 'You won't believe it, you won't believe it,' " says Kamali, elated that Simon's songs complemented the messages she conveys in the film.

That decided, Kamali exorcised much of the dialog and replaced some of it with Simon's songs: "My New Boyfriend," "Tired of Being Blonde," and "Can't Give It Up." "This is so much a woman's piece, and the music is so clearly perfect," says Kamali.

The video shows model Audrey Matson in a range of emotions, from indecision to delight, dismay, chagrin, happiness, love, and embarrassment— all the while wearing clothes from Kamali's fall collections for OMO and Jones Apparel Group.

Of the bizarre Thanksgiving meal, which features "beyond ethnic" foods like blue coffee and orange broccoli, and a frowzy-haired mother who thinks she is a "decorator," Kamali explains, "No matter who you are today, everybody has a funny background or something in their past that they're embarrassed by. This is just saying that's the way it is."

After two years of doing her own videos, Kamali and her staff have honed a system that enables them to work fast on a set to produce a professional-looking piece. She hired a professional film

"Beyond ethnic" Thanksgiving from Kamali's video

crew that had never worked in the fashion business before and was determined to show them she could come in on time and on budget. "So many people outside of fashion think fashion people are prima donnas and flakes. I wanted them to see we were professional. They couldn't believe how well we worked," she says proudly.

Filming entirely at the Palladium, she took advantage of the club's dance floor, Francesco Clemente mural, and Kenny Scharf psychedelic rec room for her sets. And the furniture? Kamali emptied her apartment and her studio to supply the props.

The film is being shown twenty-four hours a day in the store window (and inside the store when open) and will appear in department store boutiques as well. And, she adds, those who see it will come back to watch it over and over.

"People won't get bored with this because there are layers of things going on," she explains. "One time they can listen to the music and another time hear the dialog. You can come back and find something different every time."

Says Kal Ruttenstein, vice-president of fashion direction for Bloomingdale's, "Every time we think Norma's gone as far as she can go, she comes up with something like this. It makes all of those runway videos we've been doing in the stores look really tired."

About the personal nature to Audrey's story, which involves her loves, disappointments, and triumphs, Kamali winces slightly. "I was in the fetal position on my bed this morning thinking about how personal it is," she says. And with typical directness, she adds, "I wanted to throw up."

—NEW YORK, 1985

If the Dress Fits...

"So," Norma Kamali asks a reporter visiting her workroom, "how many other designers have you seen in their underwear?"

Standing behind a screen, wearing black bra, panties and socks, Kamali is fitting part of her next collection for Jones Apparel Group. "I fit on myself so that I know how the clothes feel and look," she says. "I'm my best reference. I design what I want to wear in fabrics I like. I'm doing it for me, but I think there are a lot of women out there like me.

"I look at a dress and ask myself, 'Would I wear this?' and if I can say, 'Yes, I would,' then I'll put it in the line."

The fitting progresses. Kamali and a fitting model are trying on different-colored versions of the same samples. A merchandiser and pattern maker look on. Kamali criticizes one of the tops as being too big. Its sleeves are too long. The pattern maker points out that the fleece in the last collection shrank, and the same possibility exists for this top. The sleeves are left long.

Wearing a skirt, Kamali wriggles in front of the mirror and exclaims, "I hate the stitching." She pulls at the waistband. "It makes a stiff line, and I can feel it." The stitching will be changed.

As for a sheer beige dress, Kamali declares, "I wouldn't be caught dead walking down Eighth Avenue in this." The longevity of the dress is dubious.

Kamali spends each morning in this 15,000-square-foot loft on Eighth Avenue, and some part of each of these mornings is spent doing fittings. "The fitting process is very long and very tedious," says Kamali, "but for me it's the most important part of designing, because how clothes drape and feel on the body is what is important in the end."

Yet before clothes can be created, they must be conceived. Kamali says she gets her ideas from three sources: her imagination, her staff, and from fittings.

Of her own imagination, Kamali says, "When you're in this business you think about what you do all the time, and ideas come to you all the time."

As for her staff, she says, "I have a rule in my company that everyone, and I mean everyone, whether they clean the bathroom or are in high positions of responsibility, must write me a letter once a week and tell me anything they want to tell me—personal feelings or ideas they have for the company.

"Getting that information from them will either reinforce an idea I have or give me ideas about what the customer may need. I mean, they're in the store all day. They talk to the customers."

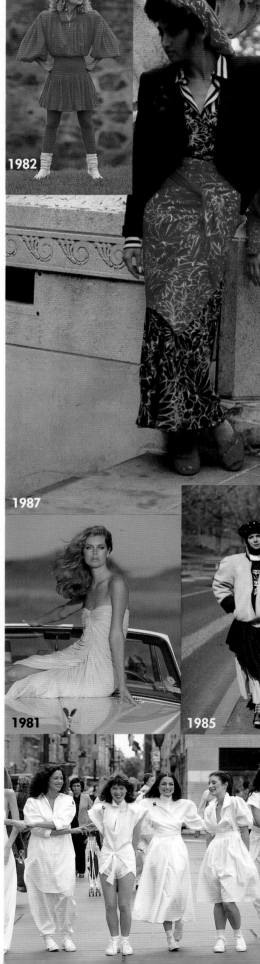

1982

1987

1981

1985

1982

1983

1978

981

1984

1982

"When you're designing, you have to consider the economy, and how much wealth people want to show on the street. I like extravagance, but clothes and jewelry can still be wonderfully exciting and fun without diamonds and rubies."

1980

1981

Kamali, 1984

The fittings, she says, "are very creative and very productive because I may fit one piece and from that one get ideas for six others." Once an idea gels, Kamali writes down a description of it. "Even if I only write three words," she says, "I find it's better than sketching because a sketch limits the possibility of where an idea could go."

To explain this concept, Kamali gives this example: There is a detail that repeats throughout the new sportswear collection so that when people put things together there is a connection. That de-

tail is pearlized buttons very closely spaced on tape made of the same fabric as the item.

"When I had the idea I wrote 'Pearlized buttons repeated in the decoration and detail.' If I'd taken the time to draw out how I wanted the buttons, I would have been stuck. Instead, I told my merchandiser, 'Listen, I have this idea for buttons. These are the kind I want, and this is the spacing I want.' She's there to facilitate the idea for me. The next day she'll bring me lots of tape

and buttons and I'll see how it looks."

Following Kamali's instructions, samples are made. Sample makers for both her OMO and licensed sportswear collections are located in her loft, so work progresses swiftly. Kamali does not sketch until a piece is made. This sketch becomes "a reference to the attitude, gesture, feeling, and movement of the garment," she says. "I'll sketch it with the personality I want it to have."

The "personality" of the collection will be reflected in the season's video, which is conceived simultaneously. "The more things you do, the more they stimulate the other things you do." The creative process behind "making videos and making clothes is the same," she says.

According to Kamali, creating is "the biggest rush." "I'm sure it's what drugs are like," she says. "I have never been into drugs because I'm addicted to designing. I take in stimuli from my life experience and then I take a part of myself and give it out, let go of it. And then I see it become something. All of a sudden you see this thing you've created, and the excitement, the high, is so wonderful that you want to do it again—right away."

The one "problem" Kamali says she's had with the creative process is that "I've always felt designing is a selfish experience.

"I've always questioned what kind of serious contribution we are making here in fashion. I mean, there are people who do things for other people that are profound and wonderful, and I always felt a little bit of embarrassment about the quality of what I do. I mean, is this really all that important?"

Kamali came to terms with the meaning of her work when she came to understand that "clothes really do give people a certain kind of joy. It may not be saving someone's life, but it does maybe save a day, or an evening, and make them feel a little bit better about themselves."

And her work, Kamali says, brings joy and meaning to her own life. "The advice that's been given to me over the years as my business has grown is to hire assistant designers. I hear this and say, 'What, are you kidding me? My dream all my life has been to do my own designing. Now that I'm doing it and my business is getting bigger, I'm not going to design? I'm going to let other people have all the fun?' No way."

—NEW YORK, 1985

"I think my clothes relate to the times we live in—and to the American woman's needs. That means being healthy, active, and very sexy. And that's what the clothes are about."

1983

1983

1985

OSCAR

Oscar de la Renta has always been a Ladies' man in the courtly European tradition—and both he and his Continental-flavored collections revel in femininity. For years his signature was ruffles, but in the Eighties he forsook them in favor of sleeker silhouettes that are still utterly and unabashedly female, since the couture-trained de la Renta has always known how to cut a curve. For those who love the haute aura but not the haute prices of his luxe ready-to-wear and furs, the de la Renta name appears on a wide range of products from the less expensive Miss O collection to loungewear and accessories. His namesake perfume is a continual top seller.

The Dominican-born designer—now a firmly entrenched New Yorker—enjoys a lavish lifestyle that has been as carefully chronicled as his collections. His awareness of his well-heeled customers' way of life is attributed by many to his late wife, Françoise, with whom he shared a talent for entertaining and creating comfort-filled homes that attracted their BP friends like lodestars. After her death in 1983, Oscar was "adopted" by a worldwide coterie of Françoise's women friends, who say they treasure his friendship, find his flirty ways irresistible, and love the way he dances.

DE LA RENTA
Fashion's Gentle Lothario

Marie-Hélène de Rothschild

OSCAR DE L'AMOUR

Hello, my sweet," a voice croons through the telephone. "When do we dine, my beloved? My car will be at your house at seven-thirty." Oscar de la Renta smiles with comfortable intimacy, slipping down into his chaise, and looks off dreamily, imagining the eager feminine face on the other end of the phone. He has just made a dinner date, and yet another woman in the world is ecstatic.

When he is with her, he will fix on her, and her alone, the merry grin that crinkles his soft brown eyes, a grin spiced with naughty, glamorous irony. His fingers will brush with admiration the stone on her necklace, as he finally kisses her moistly on the cheek. He will tease her, perhaps a bit too relentlessly,

then coax and cajole her to good humor again. They will discuss menus, flowers; he will pause to nip a wilted bloom from a plant. Although he is one of the canniest, most efficient maîtres de maison, he will convince her tenderly that he needs advice and supervision, leaving her delirious, for this, after all, is one of the things women want most from a man.

The result of Oscar de la Renta's exquisite courtship with his women is an uncommon but utterly desirable mix of edgy desire, easy familiarity, and the cozy maternal urge. He doesn't demand—he seduces. His business may be comparable in size and complexity to those of their husbands, but all of those pressures are lost over lunch, dinner, or the many chatty phone conversations throughout the day. To his women—

mother hen Grace Dudley, Alma Vicini, Annette Reed, Marie-Hélène de Rothschild, Mica Ertegun, Casey Ribicoff, Evangeline Bruce, Hélène Rochas, Marella Agnelli, Nancy Kissinger, Naty Abascal—he is handsome, sexy, but most of all, they say, a good, caring friend.

"A woman should be tremendously spoiled by a man. If you love someone, you want to spoil her, anyway." He is sitting, completely relaxed, in his favorite slouchy chair in his small study. It is the chair—oversized, allowing him almost to recline—in which he reads at night, watches television, and talks on the telephone constantly, all under the jealously watchful scrutiny of Zazie, his tiny Yorkshire terrier. When he arrived home from the office, he threw off his

Evangeline Bruce

Marella Agnelli

Naty Abascal and Grace Dudley

Nancy Kissinger

Casey Ribicoff

Hélène Rochas

Annette Reed

Mica Ertegun and Alma Vicini

Pat Buckley

jacket and buttoned on a navy cashmere cardigan with holes in the elbows, enough to melt any woman's heart.

"Probably because I am Latin I have a different point of view: There is a sense of security a man should bring to a woman, a moral backing," he admits. "That's something they have to do for each other. For Latin men, it's much easier for them to misbehave, because they're not so shy in expressing their feelings. And when they misbehave, they can do it worse than any other men. They all cheat on their wives, but love the feeling of the home. When I do something wrong," he says cautiously, and with a smile, "it doesn't really mean that much."

His lavish romanticism, so rare in men, intoxicates his women. "He is irresistible," says Casey Ribicoff. "One time when we were in the Dominican Republic, my breakfast tray was delivered, looking perfect and lovely, and Oscar marched in right behind it with a leaf from his garden. He said, 'Smell this, my sweetheart,' and it was his perfume. Can you imagine anything more romantic in the morning?"

Says Hélène Rochas, "He's an especially good friend to women because he protects them. Oscar is someone who has a profound curiosity about life—he adores it and is never, ever blasé. Everything is new for him, and I find that terrific."

"He's got one thing, above all, that's irresistible—he's got a twinkle in his eye," says Marie-Hélène de Rothschild. "He has an enormous vitality and he's always full of energy and full of little attentions for each friend. He goes out of his way to give pleasure to a friend. He's a masculine person, not a feminine one. He gives every woman the feeling that he's really interested in her—and it's genuine, it's true."

Most of Oscar de la Renta's women

were friends of his late wife, Françoise, who left him with an intricate circuit of interdependencies and who indulged his acute social instincts. She soothed his discomfort with solitude by surrounding him with people; she established a domestic model that he adopted as his own. Françoise's consuming preoccupation with Oscar was a joke of sorts among his friends, who, nevertheless, were brainwashed with this idée fixe—make Oscar happy, take care of Oscar.

"It would be much more difficult for a woman to develop this kind of friendship independently," he says, referring to the legacy of camaraderie with women that Françoise left him. "If you are a married man it is difficult to be friends with your wife's friends. But I never in my life liked to be alone. For many years I lived by myself, but I so much prefer the company of people. I'm a Cancer, you see," says de la Renta, who was born on July 22, 1932, "and we're homemakers. The most important thing is the home. I left my family's home when I was seventeen and until I was thirty-five I never had another home—I had a roof, but not a home. Then I married Françoise, and I created a home.

"Now that she's gone, I don't want to change my life; I want to keep living the way I do. I realize now how long it takes for a woman to run a house. I have three girls from the Dominican Republic helping me, and their problems are my problems. But all the little sins! The shirts are not done right, a linen pillowcase lost or torn. I don't enjoy calling the laundry to complain that the sheets are incomplete, but you have to do it.

"I do most of my telephoning from my car, with my new toy, my phone," he says. "I call the butcher, the florist, the fish market. It's not really very American for a man to run a house, but European men in a sense are more involved. Gianni Agnelli orders the food in his house. For a man, it's sort of amusing, a creative job, in a way."

Oscar de la Renta's perception of women is a heady potion of sensuality and good sense, of prescience and puzzlement. Friendship is the basis for the relationship, and beyond that is a certain rich mystery.

"First of all, a woman must be intelligent," he says flatly, "because intelligence, even a strong, challenging kind of intelligence, makes life more interesting. I would hate to be married to a dull woman. But by 'strong' I don't mean a woman who lacks femininity. Every woman must be very soignée, very well-groomed. I love to see a woman whose nails have not been polished in twenty-five different ways, and whose makeup from the morning is not repasted over. And it is very important how a woman smells; it's part of her personality. I hate when a woman changes fragrance, because she smells like someone else."

Mutual dependence is the heart of friendship, de la Renta believes. He loves to be needed, and realizes that for most people, to be called upon to help and support can inspire strong devotion. There is a certain gentillesse in him that women seek in men. "He has a great knowledge of the world, a sympathy, a compassion, an empathy with so many ideas," says Dudley. "He certainly makes life more interesting."

But if dependence is the heart of friendship, sensuality, to de la Renta, is the electricity that makes it beat. "It's wonderful if you have a lover and that lover is your friend," he observes. "It's another dimension to friendship. You can be lovers and not friends, and friends and not lovers. Not very often do they happen together. Many people go through life without ever knowing what love is all about."

Precisely this sensuality draws Oscar's women to him, for each and every one, however hesitantly, says he is handsome, sexy, physically desirable. They love the steamy, stormy torrent of feelings.

"I am extremely jealous," he declares. "Jealousy is one of the worst, the lowest emotions, real jealousy of the present, but also of the past. Just the fact that someone sort of shared certain feelings, shared an intimacy you feel should belong only to you," he says, explaining the retroactive sense of possessiveness that plagues a lover. "But I am getting better."

His teasing and his pranks, he admits, make relationships lighter, more bearable, even when he goes overboard, which he believes he sometimes does. "Sometimes I want to say something and I make a half joke to express a sentiment not otherwise easy to express, either of love or critique," he says.

Oscar the Lover surely struggles with his feelings, working through the complicated romantic tangle, calling upon his women to help him through the haze.   —NEW YORK, 1984

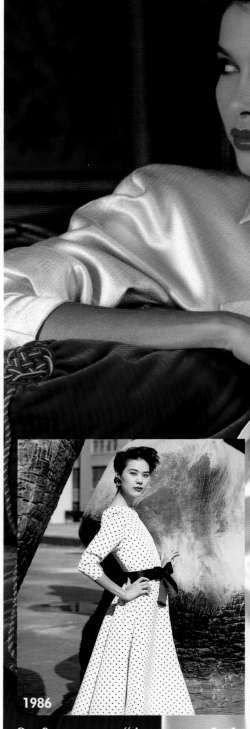

1986

On fragrance: "As a man, I always look at what a woman takes out of her handbag—it's like revealing a secret—and I'm always shocked when I see an ugly, plastic compact, especially for perfume. A beautiful perfume bottle is absolutely necessary."

1985

1983

1985

1983

1987

1982

OSCAR DE LA RENTA ON CAREER CHIC

Good quality, versatile, packable clothes" are what Oscar de la Renta says a woman needs for business. "She should be able to travel in them, sit at a desk in them, and go from day to evening in them.

"They should never be the 'dernier cri' of fashion," he says. "A woman who works wants a kind of uniform—the equivalent of a man's gray flannel suit. She's got to have a professional, no-nonsense attitude—without the kind of vanity that takes her two hours in the morning to be well groomed." De la Renta, however, does not advocate masculine attire. Not even pants. "I think women executives realize they don't have to dress like men."

Asked about Career Chic basics, he ticks off the following list: "Fantastic shoes and a bag, and for today's dressing, definitely a suit that can be changed with different blouses." Another item he thinks an essential luxury is a fur coat. "It not only keeps you warm, but it's much more versatile than a cloth coat—it can be put on top of everything, and it can go from day to night."

1985

1986

1980

1979

"My clothes stand for femininity and romance. I design
clothes for the real woman. In
one word, they stand for spice.
The woman who buys my
clothes, who can afford my
clothes, is an active and involved woman over twenty-five
who's sure of herself. She has
a clear understanding of her
position in life. She's a woman
in full bloom."

1980

BIRTHDAY BOY

What do you give a birthday boy like Oscar, a fellow who, as the saying goes, has everything? Well, if you're Ahmet and Mica Ertegun, you help him celebrate the occasion with a party at Café Mortimer.

According to Mica, "We wanted to see Dr. Kissinger, and he turned out to be free on Oscar's birthday." And if the evening weather was sultry, so was the jazz from the New York Hot Four. "We wanted something that didn't annoy the neighbors too much," explained Ahmet, who sang a few rousing choruses with the group and danced with all the Ladies. The Erteguns, the Reeds, Irith Landeau, and others will be joining de la Renta soon for a cruise off the southern Turkish coast.

Just how old was the evening's guest of honor? "Fifty-three," said Oscar. "And don't I look better than all the others?" —NEW YORK, 1985

Mary McFadden, Jerzy Kozinski, Nancy Kissinger, and Barbara Howar

The Birthday Boy and Irith Landeau

Above: The New York Hot Four;
left: Mica Ertegun and William Paley

LITTLEST OSCARS YET

If it wasn't actually a marriage made in heaven, it was certainly a sublime enough union, as Ladies' delight Oscar de la Renta got together with Barbie at a gala held by her creator, Mattel, at the Waldorf-Astoria Hotel. The toy company, which is the largest single manufacturer of female clothing in the world, creates 50 million tiny apparel items a year, and now some of them will be Oscars.

"The Barbie is Shangri-La. She never gets old and she has the perfect figure," explained her gallant swain of his new lady friend, who is twenty-six. The four outfits he's created are extravagant entrance makers adapted from his signature collection, and they were shown in their full-scale versions at the predinner presentation. Indeed, according to Oscar, "The little girls who are going to be buying Oscar de la Renta for Barbie will be my future customers." And Mattel's advertising campaign, which stresses Barbie's independence and her value as a role model for young girls, wasn't lost on the designer. "Imagine," he said, "Barbie's had the same boy friend for twenty-five years and she's not married to him. She's a very determined girl." —NEW YORK, 1985

Genie Francis, Cathy Lee Crosby, Barbie's dressmaker, Rebecca Holden, Suzette Charles, and Drew Barrymore (*front*)

OSCAR DE LA GINZA

O scar de la Renta, it seemed, was everywhere. As soon as he arrived in Tokyo at the end of a whirlwind business trip—six shows in three cities in ten days—his friends who were already there began to call, saying, in effect, "We couldn't ignore the fact that you were coming. Your picture is everywhere—in all the stores, in the streets—gigantic, like King Kong!"

It was an all-out effort by the Mitsukoshi department stores to make Oscar's presence felt in Japan—a campaign that was apparently effective: On the train, en route to Kyoto, Oscar was besieged by children asking for his autograph.

There were ten people to meet Oscar's party of five at the Tokyo airport, and for each of the six fashion shows (two each in Nagoya, Tokyo, and Osaka) he estimates "there were crews of eighty or a hundred people ready to carry out whatever I told them."

However, while Oscar speaks four languages, Japanese is not among them, and he occasionally had to resort to sign language, especially with the choreographer for the show. "He understood me," he reports, "and then I have learned a few Japanese words—like 'fast, fast' and 'please.'"   —TOKYO, 1977

Like some Big Brother of fashion, Oscar de la Renta looms over the Ginza from the facade of Mitsukoshi

THE SELF-STYLED WORLD OF OSCAR DE LA RENTA

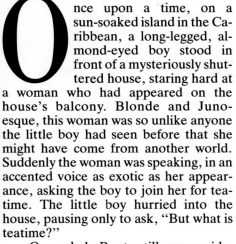

Once upon a time, on a sun-soaked island in the Caribbean, a long-legged, almond-eyed boy stood in front of a mysteriously shuttered house, staring hard at a woman who had appeared on the house's balcony. Blonde and Juno-esque, this woman was so unlike anyone the little boy had seen before that she might have come from another world. Suddenly the woman was speaking, in an accented voice as exotic as her appearance, asking the boy to join her for teatime. The little boy hurried into the house, pausing only to ask, "But what is teatime?"

Oscar de la Renta still seems wide-eyed as he describes what he says was "my first vision of a European woman." And the details of his encounter with his uncle's Russian mistress in his native Santo Domingo, as he enumerates them with the simple grace of a person telling a fairy tale, seem singularly appropriate to a designer best known for opulently romantic clothes.

"You know, I have a very bad memory, but I can even remember what she smelled like," says de la Renta. "It opened up visions of other worlds. Most of the boys from Santo Domingo wanted to go to the States to be educated; I knew I wanted to go to Europe." The fact that he is now established in the United States is an irony with which the designer is comfortable. The childhood fantasies of Paris as the sophisticated mecca of the arts have yielded to the feeling that it is, after all, "a stale and in-bred city." And although there are those who say de la Renta's designing finger is solidly on the pulse of European fashion, he says firmly, "I am an American designer," and adds, with grave sincerity, "I love this country. I couldn't have done what I've done anywhere else."

That achievement is considerable. Since de la Renta showed his first collection on Seventh Avenue for Jane Derby in 1965, his ascent has been unusually smooth. Fifteen years later, with partner Jerry Shaw, he was heading a designing empire taking in over $12 million in ready-to-wear, and receiving a 3 to 10 percent royalty on a range of licensed products grossing well over $100 million.

Certainly de la Renta has passed his American businessman's exams with flying colors. Retailers praise his knowledge of what will work in the American market. He seems to have realized successfully that "vision of other worlds"—the sense of aristocratic luxury and European refinement—of which he caught a glimpse as a child.

His New York apartment—which de la Renta describes as "a nineteenth-century retreat from the demanding life outside"—is actually a timeless mélange of Regency, French Empire, and earlier Portuguese, Spanish, and French furniture, set off against a background of red panne velvet and Orientalist paintings. A guest list for one of the architecturally detailed de la Renta soirées is usually drawn from a transcontinental roster flecked with aristocratic names. The women who buy his top-priced ready-to-wear are often the same ones who make regular pilgrimages to Paris to shop the couture.

In impeccably tailored suits, de la Renta moves through this rather Proustian world, and the less delicate environs of Seventh Avenue, with the suave ease of a Hispanic Fred Astaire. In a business that is not known for its insistence on etiquette, de la Renta maintains a courtly bearing. Business associates comment on his extraordinary calm under pressure, and de la Renta says, "When I'm very, very nervous, I sing." When he was mugged outside 550 Seventh Avenue, where his showroom is, he simply smiled broadly, handed over his money, and politely asked the thieves if he could keep his money clip, as his wife had given it to him and would be very angry if he lost it. The thieves let him keep the clip and told him, "You're a cool dude, man." (De la Renta, clearly pleased with the phrase, repeats it twice when he tells the story.)

"Obviously, my success has given me an assurance I wasn't born with," says de la Renta. "I've had a stuttering problem all my life, and I'm still painfully shy on the telephone. If I think the person knows who I am, I'm fine. But if they don't, I'm very, very shy."

De la Renta has been struggling for that self-assurance from the time of his childhood in Santo Domingo. Although he speaks of the island with romantic fondness—and compares it to the enchanted, lushly mystical world of Gabriel Garcia Marquez's *One Hundred Years of Solitude*—he admits that the early years were not without anxieties.

The son of an insurance executive ("not rich, not poor") and the only boy

among seven children, he says he was "terribly spoiled. All the girls were really like mothers to me. Of course, I was allowed much less freedom than the other boys." His mother dressed him in fancy children's clothes she purchased during periodic shopping trips to Havana, and today he complains, with a slight gesture of embarrassment, that he was forced to wear shorts to school for a longer time than anyone else, "even though I was the tallest in the class. Everyone used to call me 'stork legs.' "

De la Renta's affection for the opulently esthetic was always apparent, it seems. As an altar boy in the Catholic Church he was enamored of "the pomp of it all—I'd love to have been a cardinal." But he decided the esthetic outweighed the spiritual in his soul and, encouraged by a priest who had befriended him, planned to become an artist, a source of some contention among members of his family.

"My mother encouraged me; my father was not much for it. He wanted me to go into the business." De la Renta adds that he was "always very much my mother's son. I was always slightly reserved with my father; I felt I was probably not what he expected a son to be."

Acting upon a "tremendous craving to get away from home," de la Renta convinced his parents to let him attend art school in Madrid. At twenty, he says, he was "embarrassingly immature," unused to independence, and "so dazzled by everything, as soon as I hit my room at night, I cried." To avoid the solitude of his pension he would stay out nights as late as possible, making the rounds with the flamenco players.

His second year in Madrid found him malnourished, making little headway as an artist, and being firmly urged by his father to return to Santo Domingo and the insurance business. It was at that time, de la Renta says, he started doing fashion illustrations, first for Herrera and Ollero in Madrid, then for Castillo at Lanvin in Paris. By the early Sixties he was in the States, designing for Elizabeth Arden, then Jane Derby, and finally under his own name.

For a long time, he says, "I kept the notion that I was doing fashion to make enough money to paint, probably out of guilt. Even after I'd come to America, I felt somehow I'd cheated in the middle of the way."

From the beginning of his American career de la Renta's professional name was illuminated by the famous clients who cultivated him and who found in the designer not only a man who knew how to dress them flatteringly, but also an engaging and socially acceptable weekend and dinner guest.

Of course, it's ultimately the designer, not the bon vivant, who defines de la

BEHIND DE LA RENTA'S OWN CLOSED DOORS

In Oscar de la Renta's apartment, interior designer Bob Denning's armoire principle is at work. Built out from the corner of a room is a small but workable closet for suits, shoes, socks, and ties, which hang to the right of the shoes. Beside this space are two more French doors that open to reveal neatly stacked shirts, scarves, sweaters, and belts. A simple basket holds odds and ends. Nearby stands de la Renta's must: a valet. "I hate to have clothes thrown around, especially in a small space." About his complete dressing corner, he says, "I get dressed very fast and like to have everything in front of me, not to waste time." De la Renta's terracotta-colored bathroom includes a good-sized stall shower with multiple water jets and two Japanese touches in a corner: "I sit on a small seat and shave in the shower without a mirror"; the bucket is used to rinse after shaving. —NEW YORK, 1980

OSCAR'S NEW ADDITION

Oscar de la Renta has given a home to a nine-month-old baby abandoned on a garbage heap in Santo Domingo. The boy, called Moises by Oscar, after the biblical patriarch found in a basket, was born prematurely and apparently abandoned by his family two days after his birth. Oscar arranged for his lengthy hospitalization and is building a wing onto his Santo Domingo home for the child and his nanny. "He's susceptible to every disease and so I can't leave him in the orphanage," says de la Renta, referring to the boys' orphanage with which he is involved. "The best thing was to give him a home with me." For how long? "Till he's twenty-one and can manage on his own," answers Oscar.

—NEW YORK, 1985

Renta's reputation. And he's pleased with his current output. "Looking back at things I did in the Sixties, I was probably more daring," he says, "but the clothes weren't in as good taste. One thing I've learned since then is to edit."

De la Renta believes "there are two classes of designers—those who make such a strong impact on a certain period that it's difficult to get out of it, and the survivors," and he says he hopes he's in the latter category.

Some retailers privately say that de la Renta borrows the most successful trends from Europe and adapts them for the American market, a charge that enrages the designer. "It's pure nonsense, this America versus Europe thing," he says. He is eager to point out that a suit from a recent collection looks very much like something Givenchy did later for his couture, and says, with a trace of a pout, "If I had stayed in Paris—well, there are as, or even less, talented people doing very well there—I think I probably would be head of one of the houses. But I wouldn't trade places."

De la Renta admits without hesitation that he's very competitive. "You have to be in a business like this," he says. "Sometimes I try to restrain my anger and not be jealous of others. Even as privileged as an outsider might think I am, you always think, 'Why is this happening to someone else, not me?' I try not to think in those terms."

Close de la Renta watchers say the designer has curbed those tendencies. "As his affluence has increased, he's become far more relaxed, easier with himself," says his friend Bill Blass. "Success hasn't been a curse for him; it's improved him."

But somewhere behind the entrepreneur and host par excellence is, de la Renta says, a brooding romantic. He can often lapse into abstracted, fantasizing silence with no provocation, he says. He describes himself as "painfully romantic," has a marked fondness for Eastern mysticism (at one point he considered converting to Islam) and novelist Lesley Blanch (who has "the same romantic attachment to the mysteries of the Middle East"), and says he would like to have been the explorer Richard Burton, who sought the source of the Nile in the nineteenth century.

Correspondingly, de la Renta says one thing he misses in his life—which is, to a great extent regimented by social and professional demands—is the opportunity to travel impulsively. "I think there's something wonderful about standing in a new town in the middle of a street," he says. "Sometimes I fantasize about the caravan, being sort of a nomad."

He stops to consider for a moment and adds, "Of course, I'd have to be a nomad who had a wonderful tent, wonderful food, and wonderful carpets on the floor. You know—like *The Arabian Nights*." —NEW YORK, 1979

Oscar and Françoise after their 1967 marriage

O, What a Match

"I never thought I would marry," admits Oscar. "But I'm very happy." "I never thought I'd feel like marrying again," says Françoise. "But it's great. Now I'm pushing everyone I know into it."

This is the way Mr. and Mrs. Oscar de la Renta talk about their recent marriage, on Halloween 1967. The night before, Oscar had said to Françoise, "What are you doing for lunch tomorrow?" Instead of lunching they went down to City Hall.

She is the former Françoise de Langlade, who was editor of French *Vogue*. Born in Paris, where her mother and grown son still live, she became an American citizen while she was married to her second husband, a member of the diplomatic service in Washington. Once she worked for Diana Vreeland on *Harper's Bazaar*, where she pressed dresses for Louise Dahl Wolfe to photograph. In 1953 she started working for French *Vogue*; she became fashion editor and moved up to editor-in-chief.

When Françoise was at *Vogue* in Paris, Oscar was working for Castillo. "I remember one day before the Castillo collection opened I took a blue coat over to *Vogue*'s offices—there was Bill Klein taking photos and Françoise was at the sitting. She was very nice and condescending." He winks at Françoise. "Then we met again when I was working at Elizabeth Arden. One day I came out of the door and there was Françoise over from Paris. I asked her out for dinner. She said, 'No, but maybe cocktails.'

"Some time went by before we met again—this time in Paris when I went with C.Z., Mingo, and Winston. There were many parties given for C.Z."

"And at all those parties," continues Françoise, "I was always sitting beside Oscar. One night Jacqueline de Ribes gave us tickets for the ballet. That was our first date—like grown-ups." Then the commuting started, for two years.

What happens when a fashion editor marries a fashion designer? Well to hear Françoise tell it, Oscar is doing a fine job of creating a new image for her. "I used to dress in a very strict way. Now I'm learning to dress more amusingly. I never would have thought of dressing like this two years ago."

—NEW YORK, 1968

CONNECTICUT YANKEE

A wooded road scattered with persimmon leaves leads to Brook Hill Farm, the de la Renta country home in Kent, Connecticut. It sits high on a hill, in a clearing amid seventy acres—gray-shingled, white-shuttered, a robust and rather cozy house, even from the outside.

Oscar, wearing corduroys and a Shetland sweater, has taken to his trac-

tor by the barn, accompanied by a barking collie and two yapping Yorkshire terriers. Recently twelve black sheep were added to the growing menagerie, which includes a cat as well as horses.

"This is real country, not Southampton," says Françoise. "There are no other houses around at all."

It's strange—if not impossible—to imagine the de la Rentas as two recluses. They are among the rare breed who could make Siberia an IN spot, let alone

Kent, Connecticut. "The whole dream here is not to move from the house but to have friends come to us. But it's organized—no dropping in from door to door. We loathe that. We don't do it in the city, so why should we do it here?"

The living room reflects their love of luxury and a confidence in mixing color and well-ordered clutter: green and violet papered walls, quilt-covered tables, stacks of books everywhere, plump Victorian sofas, and red taffeta curtains,

The living room with well-ordered clutter

The master bedroom

Horses, sheep, and dogs complete the scene.

Brook Hill Farm, the de la Renta weekend retreat

A corner for games

Doing chores, *above*, and out inspecting the grounds, *right*.

unlined to let the sun in. And, because they often show movies here in the winter, lots of blankets all over the place. Any entertaining is usually on Saturday night, with no more than four or six for dinner, "and mostly friends in the area."

The de la Renta country house, like the city apartment, is run with an almost legendary meticulousness. Their cook— a young woman from Oscar's native Dominican Republic, where he has another house—accompanies them from the city.

Oscar settles by the fire and talks about his ideal day. "I like to ride in the morning on the trails, come back to the house around eleven, work in the garden, and have lunch before taking a walk in the afternoon."

It's obvious that the de la Rentas have gotten country entertaining down to a T. This Sunday's luncheon menu: shepherd's pie, salad, cheese and fruit, followed by espresso and chocolates.

Some other country touches:
FOOD: "Vegetables from the country—tomatoes and asparagus. And when in season, corn, corn, corn on the cob until you get fed up with it."

WINE: "Cold Beaujolais—it has the coolness of white and the warmth of red."

TABLE SETTINGS: "Much less dainty than in the city . . . tablecloths sewn from scarves from Pierre Deux, brown and white pottery from the South of France, and a table that is a bit more crowded— bread and butter in baskets and cruets on the table."

CLOTHING: As for packing for a de la Renta country weekend: "Guests are told to bring a pair of jeans, just so they won't pack their Saint Laurents or their Balenciagas." Or their Oscar de la Rentas.
　　　　—KENT, CONNECTICUT, 1976

Emanuel Ungaro has remarked that everything he does is, at heart, sensual in its motivation. The very body-conscious, strategically draped and shirred little dress that over the years has become his signature is the most copied dress in fashion. Ungaro modestly describes its appeal: "It is the image of seduction." Sustaining such an image requires perseverance, and Ungaro is a man known to spend endless, exacting hours in his studio. His clothes always have a specific and visual impact, whether it's a man's striped jacket thrown over a slinky floral evening dress or the vivid, unorthodox mélange of high-voltage prints for which he has become known. His single-minded approach to fashion has proved profitable: His worldwide retail sales top $150 million (about half of which is sold in Japan) and couture sales bring in several million dollars. Even in his leisure time, Ungaro is wont to approach things with the fanaticism he lends to every pursuit. Not long ago, while wandering the countryside in his native Aix-en-Provence, he came across an ancient dilapidated farmhouse he decided he had to have, and spent most of his vacation trying to convince the farmer who owned it to part with it. He is, after all, by his own admission, a "possessed" man.

EMANUEL UNGARO
The Casanova of Paris Fashion

UNGARO: SEEKING PERFECTION

Emanuel Ungaro's eyes are his best weapon, at once probing, fierce, quizzical, and even a bit mad. Unblinking, they pierce and beguile everyone.

The couturier's eyes are also impenetrable, revealing little about the passionate drive that propelled him from his father's modest tailor shop in Aix-en-Provence to the influential fashion institution that celebrated its twentieth anniversary with the fall 1985 couture collection.

"I'm becoming more and more obsessed," says the designer intensely. "If I have one quality, it is that I am harnessed intellectually. I accomplish myself when I work. Really it's very strange," he continues, sinking into a low, modern sofa in a chamber adjacent to his Spartan work studio, "it's like being a musician. Do you think playing music is like a job to him?"

Ungaro produces ten collections a year, for couture and ready-to-wear—Parallel, Solo Donna, and Ungaro TER (knitwear). He also oversees forty-six licensing operations in the U.S., Europe, and Japan, ranging from men's wear to home furnishings.

Twenty-five years old when he began his six-year apprenticeship with Cristobal Balenciaga in 1958, Ungaro had already worked with his father and four brothers in the family tailoring business and then in small shops in Paris. "Balenciaga was strong and silent. He had enormous authority—he was undisputed," recalls Ungaro of the reclusive Spanish "monk" of Paris couture. Ungaro, who describes himself then as a "hungry lion," spent six years watching Balenciaga's every move and gesture. "I literally stood behind him twelve hours a day, sometimes seven days a week. I watched, I imitated, I just ate everything up. He was the master. I learned everything from him." Ungaro cried when he left, though it was his choice to go.

Although Balenciaga never came to one of Ungaro's fashion shows, a sore point with the designer, Ungaro still reveres his memory, in the same way Hubert de Givenchy, another Balenciaga protégé, does. (It is ironic, therefore, that Ungaro and Givenchy are particular rivals, and that sometimes they will go to the silliest lengths to antagonize each other.)

Before he went out on his own, Ungaro repaid a debt to André Courrèges, another former Balenciaga assistant, who had introduced him to Balenciaga and helped secure Ungaro his first job. Ungaro spent two seasons with Courrèges, then the most talked-about couturier in Paris, but by most accounts it wasn't a very pleasant experience, especially after some journalists speculated that much of Courrèges's short-lived success was due to his new assistant. In any case, Ungaro brushes the interlude aside, still claiming he has "no comment."

In 1965, he and his graphic-artist girlfriend, Swiss-born Sonja Knapp, scraped together a little over $5,000 and set up the house of Ungaro in a one-room studio on the Avenue Macmahon near the Étoile.

In the early years the designer was known as "Ungaro the terrorist" and the king of "Tough Chic." He once thought nothing of sending out a model in a long cloak of lace medallions, which were tied together with Ping-Pong balls and complemented by an aluminum bra, or issuing pretentious edicts proclaiming "the death of evening clothes."

"I was finding my way, learning about my emotions," he says. "I was greatly impressed by the upheaval in 1968. I thought everything in life would change. Of course, nothing did."

Now he has settled down to the "sensuous and rich" look he feels is the style for the Eighties, a distinctive approach that has been one of the most influential in recent seasons.

He has shirred, pleated, and draped his way around the bodies, and into the hearts, of an adoring and loyal couture clientele, including Marie-Hélène de Rothschild (who has been with him since his very first show), Ann Getty, Lynn Wyatt, Isabelle D'Ornano, and Jackie Onassis.

"All those lovely prints and colors," says de Rothschild. "He can mix anything, and it doesn't look as though it clashes. Going to a fitting at Ungaro is like going home—it's such a happy house. Still," she continues, "if there's a collection I don't like, I'll go straight up to him after the show and tell him, 'It's horrible,' but he always takes it nicely, as he admires my sense and knows I'd never flatter him."

"At the beginning, I was designing for the sake of design. I was making statements," says Ungaro, whose early minimal shapes in solid colors sometimes drew accusations of being too aggressive or too reminiscent of Courrèges. It was in the early Seventies that the beginnings of the distinctive Ungaro look emerged: a rich, colorful, and—to use one of his favorite words—"liquid"

1985

direction that seemed to take off around the time Ungaro says he started paying more attention to "the desires of a woman—what she wants and needs."

And what exactly does a woman want? There is a confident flash of the eyes and a twitch of a smile on his otherwise grave face. Ungaro knows. "A woman wants to seduce and be seduced," he says slowly and simply. "She wants an identity, and she wants sensuality." This is clearly one of his favorite subjects.

"I am completely passionate about women," says Ungaro. "I have this ideal of a woman. Like Anouk Aimée, she symbolizes in many ways the woman I have in mind. I dream a lot. It is impossible to make a collection unless I have dreamed it first."

Ungaro became obsessed with Anouk Aimée when he saw her in *Les Mauvaises Rencontrés* in 1955. Now Aimée is the "image" of the house, which mainly entails modeling his clothes for advertising campaigns. "It's a love affair," she declares, but then quickly adds, "I'm talking about the dresses and me." Ungaro himself seems to be as much of an enigma to her as he is to the rest of the world. "He's very kind, very generous," says Aimée, "but to work the way he does—it's just not normal."

Ungaro seems to be too compulsive to notice his fan club, typically swooning socialites so hypnotized by his dark, Latin good looks that they seldom notice he is actually on the short side of 5 feet 3 inches tall. One smitten Parisienne, a noted art dealer, was known to have pounded on his front door in the middle of the night in a vain attempt to get some attention. Elusive Emanuel pretended not to be at home.

Perhaps the ladies don't realize that Emanuel Ungaro is nothing like his tempting, often torrid confectionary creations. He is, instead, the aloof, meticulous master craftsman. Those little bits of provocatively draped silk are in fact products of his painstaking engineering skills, a precise and sophisticated science. He concocts fantasy visions of women in sumptuous mixes of prints, fabrics, and textures, but all of the while he lives a Spartan regimen that some of his following would find ridiculously austere.

By eight-thirty in the morning he is at work in his 2 avenue Montaigne headquarters, housing a ground-floor Ungaro boutique, corporate offices, and studios. He will not leave until seven or eight at night, works weekends, and rarely, he says, goes out at night.

He has never been married, though he had a long romantic relationship with Sonja Knapp, his business partner, until about nine years ago, when they parted on friendly terms. She has continued to design most of the Ungaro fabrics, playing a key part in the trademark prints-on-prints look, and oversees all the Japanese licensing operations. She remains a part owner of the House of Ungaro.

Ungaro wears the same uniform every day: a white smock made especially for him by one of his brothers, who continued the tailoring trade in Aix-en-Provence. With or without the smock,

Ungaro wears only black, gray, beige, or white. He is inexplicably fond, however, of red shoes.

His exacting senses are not happy until they can sniff out a sense of perfection, whether it is in a country landscape of Provence, where he keeps a home, or "right before a show, for about three minutes, when the mannequins are all ready." Alas, soon after the show he decides it wasn't quite right after all, and as usual, he reports to work the very next day to start all over again.

He loves the idea of perfection so much that he lulls himself to sleep by humming a segment of a Beethoven string quartet because, he says, "It is an achievement of perfection in harmony. This fascinates me."

If he weren't a designer he would have been a conductor because of his love of music. He remembers instantly what music he listened to twenty years ago when he was designing his very first collection: *Cosi Fan Tutti* by Mozart.

Ungaro is the brooding sort who virtually torments his soul for his craft. "It gets more and more difficult every day. The pressure is more important." Anxious to be understood, he continues, "I do not care so much about growing bigger and bigger. I care about growing better, inside, intellectually." The fruits of his labor do not seem to interest him. "I have what I have." He shrugs, sweeping his arm to indicate his offices.

However, he is relentless in his desire to create an ambience—"an environment, not just clothes"—but pledges never to lose what his former assistant, Giorgio Armani, calls his "religious dedication to fashion." "I love to work," he says simply. "I don't know if I am a success or not, and I do not mean to be arrogant when I say this. I haven't achieved all that I have in my mind.

"When I'm alone in my studio in the early morning, I'm thinking of the conditions that were mine when I started, without money, without connections. The emotion I feel is enormous. Almost all the people I had then are still with me. I feel proud of the talent in our house. I am not here alone, you know."

It is during these hours, he says, that he is most taken with the process of design. "I am there with the white toile, and it is nothing," he says softly. "It's frightening and exhilarating at the same time. I am in front of all the possibilities. I do not think my story is finished yet."

—PARIS, 1985

1984

1986

1979

1984

1984

1982

1984

1987

1985

A Woman and a Man

Emanuel Ungaro is a master of the artful tease, as adept at delivering passionate and flowery compliments as he is at abruptly closing up the drawbridge to his metaphoric castle. But nowadays, when the women come knocking, he's probably elsewhere. For some time, Ungaro has been lavishing his tender attentions on enigmatic French actress Anouk Aimée. She wears his clothes and his perfume and is rarely seen in Paris or New York without him. In his company, she shows a coquette's appetite for flattery, which he frequently delivers in an orotund style that borders at times on the outrageous.

She is visibly upset when she's not around him. She looked ecstatic, however, at a recent dinner here at La Grenouille when he sat next to her and spent the night caressing her back. At the end of the evening, he took her big black scarf and enveloped her in it tenderly.

In conversation, the voluble Ungaro takes the lead and she follows, echoing his words and phrases, even correcting his English, but volunteering mysteriously little herself. They sometimes spar, but the balance seems to be in his favor. At one meal in Paris, Ungaro wanted red wine and she favored white. They ordered both, and she ended up drinking both.

Ungaro, who is fifty-one, claims they first "met" when he saw her in one of her movies. He was seventeen. When, years later, she came to his studio, he said to her, *"Enfin vous voilà."* ("At last you are here.")

Aimée and Ungaro were staying at the Hotel Westbury during their week in New York. They had two big suites—separate suites—according to a source at the hotel, who declined to say whether the rooms were adjoining.

The pair is one of the most celebrated couples in Paris fashion circles at the moment, and one of the few whose love might dare to speak its name—if they were willing to be explicit about it. When he is asked a direct question about the nature of their romance, Ungaro blushes and says, "There is no answer to that," and Aimée responds crisply, "Let's take the next page." But the designer is far from reticent on the subject of his companion's fine points. "She is the most feminine and sensual woman I have ever known," he proclaims. "She makes my work more sensuous because even the way she moves, the way she walks, is very important to me."

At fifty-two, the actress's grace and beauty are undimmed. The celebrated almond eyes, best known to American audiences from the 1966 Oscar-winning film *A Man and a Woman,* are still smolderingly catlike. She moves with a feline deliberateness and assurance, stretching her slender legs, tossing her hair, and putting her hands over her mouth and laughing softly—the mannerisms of a celebrated coquette who is a consummate mistress of the art of flirtation.

She is also a great advertisement for

Anouk Aimée and Emanuel Ungaro

to keep the mystery, the secret of life. In the Mediterranean, a woman doesn't talk as much. It's difficult for me to say. You have to keep your . . ." She gestures toward her body with outspread hands, as if to indicate her inner self.

"She's very shy, even if she is a diva," Ungaro says protectively.

Aimée, who is wearing a black wool Ungaro dress with a jabot, rises from the low, modern couch where she is sitting to answer a call. She apologizes for the interruption, sitting down again and leaning forward confidently. "For a woman you can think—but you can't say it. I think it's part of femininity not to talk too much."

The two like to travel together, particularly, as Ungaro says, to Tuscany. "What I like very much also is to go to the movies together," he adds. "It is a mystery. Something is strange to me. It's not like going to the movies with a normal human being."

They also like to listen to music and are keen opera fans, favoring Verdi. "In the morning I listen to string quartets and in the afternoon opera," says Ungaro. "My dream is to be able to play the violincello. When I see a quartet playing, there's something so tense between them. It's like doing a collection. You have to make a different movement every time."

He also sounds as if he is talking about the tension between himself and Aimée. While he is always touching her, she rarely touches him—as if her holding back might maintain their balance. At one point, Ungaro rises to pick up something and stumbles in his rush back across the room. Aimée steadies him with an outstretched hand.

"We talk French, Italian, even English together," Ungaro goes on to say. "Italian is nice. It is easier to laugh in Italian than in French," he affirms. "And laughing is the most evident complicity. There is a Louise de Vilmorin story about a woman who was very jealous of another woman who was having dinner with her husband. Her friend said, 'Why? They're not doing anything,' and the first woman said, 'Exactly. They're laughing together.' "

As the interview finishes, Ungaro, with a courtly flourish, presents his Diva perfume. Seeing this, his lady leans toward him and asks, with teasing reproach, "Why didn't you give me any?"

"Because you are a diva" is his tender response. —NEW YORK, 1984

Diva, which Ungaro claims was inspired by her. During dinner, she often disappears to the ladies' room and comes back wafting great clouds of it. "Emanuel made me walk on the streets wearing it for a year before the perfume came out," she says, laughing. "It was to drum up business."

To Ungaro's courtly declarations, her response is "What can I say after all that? You know, for a woman, one has

1985

1982

1984

In 1971 Emanuel Ungaro mixed his first prints, a signature ever since, and he carried it one step further in the winter of 1972, when he mixed not only prints but also fabrics (including fur). Moving into the Eighties, Ungaro favors his long, sexy waistless dresses, his dramatic flower prints, sheer, bow-tied blouses, and his "constantly evolving" fitted jackets. Among his early favorites are the short bloomers and fitted vest he created in 1968, which he believes "sum up the youth and energy of the period."

1982

1987

1984

1984

1986

1985

1986

1984

1979

1977

1981

Seduction with Diva

Ungaro with the Diva lineup and the pleated dress that inspired the bottles, *right*

Emanuel Ungaro is counting on his Diva fragrance to strike women with the force of a sexual assault. "With the bottle, the atmosphere surrounding the perfume, and the perfume itself, I must eventually rape them," says Ungaro. "The problem is winning the type of woman who's so loyal to her perfume she thinks she won't change. I must steal her by seduction and get her to identify with Diva. Can you imagine the incredible fifty-year success of Chanel No. 5? That's what I'm up against."

Ungaro describes Diva as the olfactory extension of his fashion philosophy. "For me, fashion is not merely creating dresses. I think I am more a creator of atmosphere, of phenomena. I seek to show the quality of the woman in everything she does—eating, talking, looking. I really want to help her reveal herself by the way she dresses. What I design is not 'la mode,' but a mode of behavior. Anyone can design a dress, but I am after an aura. With my collections, and now with perfume, that's what I'm working for."

Diva is being positioned as a fragrance for women with a conquering spirit. According to Ungaro, his customer is brazen and headstrong. "She knows how to control her life, and not with egoism. Everything about her is soignée, from her skin to her hair to her teeth to her voice. She has a thirst for confrontation," he says. "Diva is to the olfactory sense what my clothes are to the eyes. It is a logical extension of my fashion house, which has a particular style. The name describes not just the singer but a woman who lives like a conquistador, with flamboyance, mystery, and bravura."

Ungaro recalls that as a child in the South of France he was overwhelmed during high summer by the hot, humid scent of the earth mingled with pine needles. In a nonspecific way, he says, the fragrance crystallizes those impressions and memories.

The fragrance was created by Jacques Polge, the young "nose" who works solely for the Chanel group, of which Parfums Ungaro is a subsidiary. Hervé Garand, commercial director, describes the fragrance as a floral amber. "We wanted it to be feminine, but not passively feminine." The bottle was produced by Pochet du Courval and designed by Jacques Helleu, who works exclusively for Chanel. Its fashion equivalent, according to Ungaro, is the group of pleated silk dresses from his spring '83 couture collection.

"The success of a perfume is based on word of mouth and the seduction that operates on the woman who wears it," he reflects. "My authority is as a couturier with a fantastic sense of quality. Last year we added a less expensive line to the ready-to-wear, and the fragrance completes the strategy of reaching out to more people. They're both luxury, which is for me the contrary of vulgarity, not the contrary of poverty."

—PARIS, 1983

U NEVER HAD IT SO GOOD

Pat Lawford and Lee Radziwill were among the earliest friends to wish Emanuel Ungaro welcome to New York at his boutique launch on Madison Avenue. Doris Duke and Jackie O had made appointments earlier to buy clothes and thereby avoided the freeloader crush and mob-filled five-story opening that drew more than five hundred people.

"Up to now," Ungaro had said earlier in the day, "we have presented ourselves in the U.S. with perhaps too much discretion, too much elegance. Now it is time to change that. It is time to open up."

By 8:30 P.M. the Fashion Pack types were squeezing up and down the unfinished staircases watching Ungaro's ready-to-wear and couture fashions from the two levels, comprising 2,500 square feet and showcasing the complete Ungaro line—ready-to-wear, accessories, shoes, scarves, and jewelry, plus a men's shop. Diana Vreeland loped in wearing a large

shawl and two mini–disco bags. She had her usual surrealistic comments about the clothes. "Ummm, those brass and jewel-encrusted breastplates . . . practical, prat-i-co, I tell you."

Designed by French architect Pierre Rahoult, who also did the Ungaro Couture House and the ready-to-wear boutique on the avenue Matignon, the new shop is a near replica of the cool, modern, and mirrored Paris headquarters.

Bettina Graziani and Sophie Xuereb of Ungaro's fashion family orchestrated forty-five to a private buffet in the boutique's dining room. As young boys came to greet everyone at the U table, Vreeland yelled to Betty Bacall: "Teeth, I adore all the teeth in the room. When one sees such teeth, such smiles, one bows, don't you?"

At midnight, half the private buffet guests moved on to Regine's throbbing dance floor.

"I'm withered," said Bacall as she sauntered to a cab at 2:45 A.M.

—NEW YORK, 1977

Diana Vreeland observing Ungaro couture

Diana Vreeland observing Ungaro

Dancing the night away with Lauren Bacall

Fernando Sanchez and Diane Von Furstenberg

EMANUEL UNGARO 73

At Home in Aix-en-Provence

"hese are my roots," proclaims Emanuel Ungaro as he conducts a tour around his native Aix, a picturesque town in the middle of Provence in the South of France. "The sun, the colors, the lush countryside have all affected my work."

Although a Frenchman by birth, Ungaro is the son of Italian immigrants, and he can still bitterly recall the unveiled insults and prejudice he suffered as a child and as a young adult. "It is not very subtle, having the feelings of an im-

migrant's son," he says, drawing heavily on yet another Murati cigaret. "All my life I was forced to struggle, to prove things that other people had taken for granted. It made me competitive and vengeful. It made me always want to be number one."

Still, Ungaro is very proud of his heritage, and as he walks he rapturously points out the haunts of his youth and rattles off the important dates in the town's history. His mother lives just outside the town, and Ungaro has fashioned a simple holiday retreat from a deserted

nineteenth-century shepherd's hut next to her house. The stone cottage has only two big rooms, a downstairs study with coarse white-washed walls and a few magnificent pieces of antique Spanish furniture, and an upstairs bedroom with little more than a bed. The house stands next to a neighbor's small vineyard and overlooks a massive hilly lawn that Ungaro has let grow wild.

Beyond the ocher soil of the vineyard and the leafy mint trees stands the Mont Saint Victoire, a greenish-gray and white mound of rock that Ungaro

In the marketplace

In front of his stone cottage

suggests is the symbol of his youth and one of the keys to his personality. "It had a mystical meaning to me and to many of my generation," says Ungaro, who was born in 1933. "I've climbed to the top several times. Indeed, from the first moment I became aware it existed, when I was three or four, I knew I would have to climb it. The day I made it to the top is one of the happiest memories of my life."

Although he is aloof and sometimes humorless in Paris, Ungaro undergoes a pleasant metamorphosis in the Proven-çal sun. He cracks jokes, speaks endlessly of food and wine, gossips and reminisces. Since he is of Italian descent, he explains, he believes in a tightly knit family, and he remains close to his brothers, one of whom, René, now works with him in Paris. Another brother, he boasts, is a professor of philosophy, while another followed in his father's footsteps and became a local men's tailor. "We are all warm, emotional, and difficult," Ungaro says. "It comes from my father, who was all of those things and so much more."

The elder Ungaro came to Aix from the south of Italy in the Twenties, soon after Mussolini's rise to power. He was a dedicated anti-Fascist, and Ungaro has inherited some of his leftist views. What he remembers most about his father, who died in 1978, is his gusto and his pas-sion for art. "My father was full of ideas, of thoughts of life," he says.

But his father liked having the family around him, and he was angry when Ungaro decided, at age twenty-two, to move to Paris to ply his trade as a fashion designer. Ungaro had learned the rudiments of tailoring in his father's shop, and it was expected that one day he would take over the business. Even after his son had made a name for himself, the elder Ungaro remained a bit disappointed and unbelieving. "He really didn't care about Paris or couture or about superstar fashion designers," explains Ungaro. "He would have been content if I made men's suits in Aix. He never even realized I had become well known, and he couldn't fathom why some of his friends had actually heard of me."

—AIX-EN-PROVENCE, 1981

EMANUEL UNGARO 75

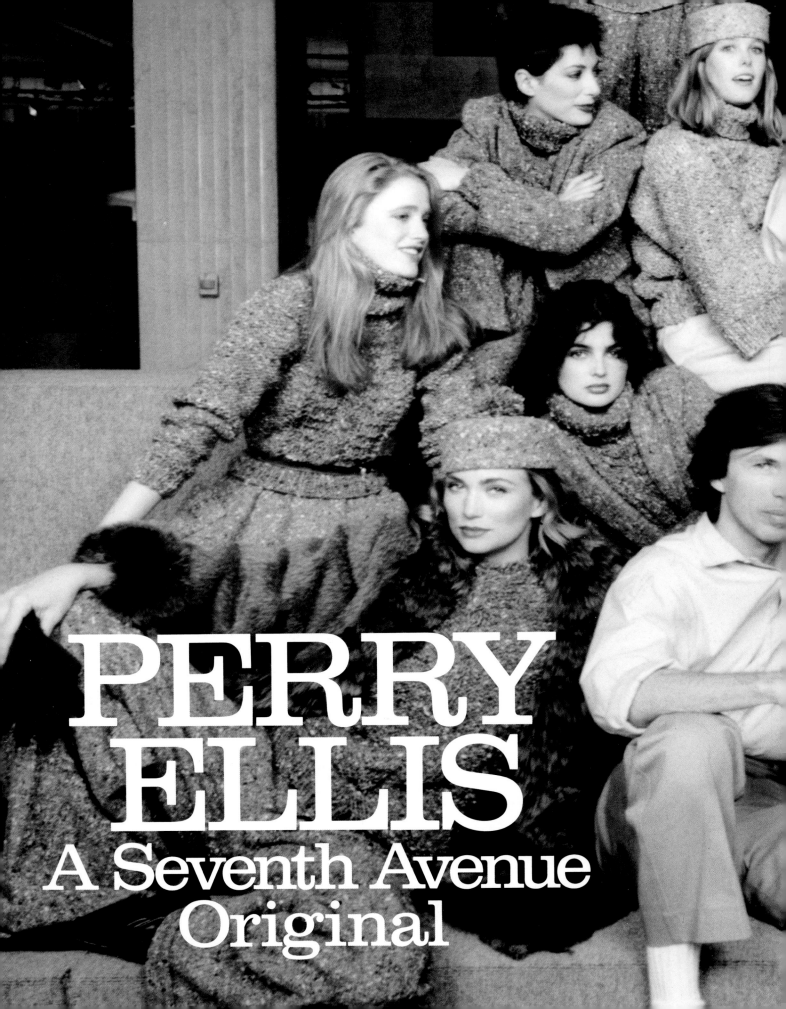

PERRY ELLIS
A Seventh Avenue
Original

Perry Ellis, who built a multifaceted fashion empire with a young and spirited approach to casual sportswear, was one of America's most important designers. His death in May 1986, at the age of forty-six, marked the end of a design career that lasted just over ten years but that left an indelible stamp on America's fashion industry. His final collection three weeks before his death was one on which he had worked with unusual intensity, doing up to 90 percent of the fittings himself. When he came out for what would be the final bow, he received a standing ovation. His efforts had produced what many critics called one of his best collections. Along with the sense of a new sophistication, it also was infused with the humor and youthful charm of his earlier work.

At his peak, Ellis created clothes that were the styles of offbeat collegians, who favored things such as brightly colored handknit sweaters, amusing elfin hats, unusual cuts, dimpled sleeves on his jackets, and bold buttons. The traditional close to his fashion shows had the designer, for a long time sporting a wild mane of hair, bounding down the runway with his models to cheers and applause of admiring retailers and friends. During his fashion ascendancy, he was called the Mr. Pop of American Fashion.

1982

1981

1984

Ellis with his "Slouch" collection

A REMAR

Perry Ellis gave women "slouchy" layers of relaxed, oversize, unconstructed shapes; whimsical cartoon-style clothes; a fashion feast of sweaters, from abbreviated body-hugging styles to tweedy handknits, witty argyles, and unique patterns; down jackets and cropped pants tucked at the hip; inventive proportions, offbeat colors, and creative fabric mixes. It was a career of

creativity that helped build the designer's name into a fashion business stretching over a broad range of products, many of them licensed. Total wholesale volume of products bearing the Ellis name is estimated to reach over $175 million in 1986, the year of his death.

A native of Portsmouth, Virginia, Ellis graduated with a bachelor's degree in business administration from the College of William and Mary in Williamsburg, Virginia, in 1961. He enlisted in the Coast Guard, served in President Kennedy's White House honor guard, and then earned a master's degree in retailing at New York University School of Retailing in 1963. Moving into retailing, he became a sportswear buyer for Miller & Rhoads in Richmond, Virginia. His experience there led him to believe that he could design better-looking clothes than those he was buying.

He once said, "I was constantly redesigning everything I saw. I would go into the showrooms and the clothes would never be right. So, I'd give them a sketch and a cutting ticket, and they'd give me the kind of clothes I wanted for the store."

In 1968, Ellis went to work for John Meyer of Norwich, a sportswear manufacturer, where he was largely responsible for merchandising. When Meyer died in 1974, Ellis joined the Vera

Companies, a division of Manhattan Industries, as vice-president of merchandising. For fall 1976 he came out of the back room and started designing under the Portfolio label. That line proved successful, and in 1978 Manhattan Industries gave Ellis a line under his own name.

He was American fashion's free spirit, the designer who unabashedly confessed that he always tried to be "different," and who often appeared to be just waiting to see what a season's key message would be so he could take a stand against it. The "slouch" look became his trademark in the early years, and loose and baggy trousers, oversize jackets, and ample skirts and sweaters set trends throughout the country. He also sold knitwear kits so home knitters could make Ellis sweaters. In 1978, Ellis also formed his own firm, Perry Ellis International, to handle licensing ventures, which included sheets, shoes, fragrance, furs, men's wear, and his American line of jeans and casual sportswear for Levi Strauss.

Ellis appeared to approach the apparel business informally. He was rarely seen wearing anything but his khaki slacks, blue button-down shirt, and Top-Siders. His relaxed style of dressing reflected his personality. (Of his own designs, he once said, "I really feel like

1984

1980

1984

KABLE CAREER

1982

1985

1982

1984

1980

1986

SWEATER DELIGHT

1984

DREAMGIRLS

1982

1981

1981

1981

1980

1981

"I really feel I'm trying to do everyday clothes that are friendly—like a new shirt that feels old and comfortable—and look like old friends hanging in your closets."

1979

1979

1982

81

I'm trying to do everyday clothes that are friendly—like a new shirt that feels old and comfortable—and look like old friends hanging in your closet.")

Yet, he was undoubtedly serious about both his career and the industry in which he functioned. During his last two years, he served as a highly effective president of the Council of Fashion Designers of America. So effective, in fact, that two days before his death, despite the viral encephalitis that had left him in a coma, the CFDA re-elected him to a third term, in obvious recognition of his past service.

Ellis also was as concerned about image as any major designer and had, like his most successful counterparts, a knack for promotion and public relations. He oversaw all of his company's advertising and made it a point to become acquainted with the country's leading fashion reporters and editors, many of whom considered Ellis a friend. "They are as important to my career as my clothes," he once said. And in a gentlemanly manner, he often wrote thank-you notes to those who covered his collections, or sent flowers or books he thought they might enjoy.

One of his great personal delights was his daughter, Tyler Alexandra Gallagher Ellis, who was born in November 1984 and lives in California with her mother, Barbara Gallagher. "My little girl is an enormous pleasure and joy to me," Ellis once said. "I never realized how important a child is, how they can make you laugh. Oh God, it's wonderful."

Ellis ran an unusual studio in which his employees were free to express themselves creatively, even allowing them time off to indulge other interests, whether they be acting or film directing. "I try to make everything available to the people who work here," Ellis explained just a month before his death. "Designing is being creative in a broad sense."

His staff was composed largely of graduates of the Parsons School of Design. He gave his assistants drawings illustrating the proportions he had in mind, rather than making detailed sketches himself. He once said, "It's very important for me to have a group of young people who are wildly talented as part of my day-to-day being." It is this staff that has been entrusted to carry on the Perry Ellis name in fashion.

—NEW YORK, 1986

Louise's Tales from Tokyo

The Chinese may think their Gang of Four are exciting, but recently I was more interested in observing the high jinks of Tokyo's Gang of Five—Peevish Perry Ellis, Gentle Giorgio Armani, Katty Karl Lagerfeld, Zapped-Out Zandra Rhodes, and Modest Madame Hanae Mori.

Imagine, if you will, my excitement at seeing those Shoguns of Style on the same runway. And imagine, if you can, the absolute ecstasy I felt at finding four or five on the same floor of the Hotel Okura, draped around my luxurious suite like so many Savage Samurai. Before the week was out, fashion rudeness would be raised to an art form, and the intrigue that ensued put my old cronies in the Hungarian court to shame.

The "best five" designers were selected by the fashion newspaper *WWD for Japan* and kept in Tokyo by the Japanese government, the *Asahi Shimbun* newspaper, the Shiseido cosmetics company, and a group of textile-industry trade associations. The week-long extravaganza cost a mere $500,000.

The week got off to a perfect start when Poor Perry was greeted at the airport by the Japanese equivalent of a Greyhound bus. Its last occupant had been Halston's crew, and Polite Perry claimed he could still "sense him." Perry then went into virtual seclusion for the rest of the week, emerging, of course, only when any reporter asked for an interview. He went to few of the social events, and seemed to spend whole days fitting his female and male mannequins.

Of course, he was a busy man. Not only did he have to look after the five models he flew over from New York (at his Japanese licensee's expense), but he had only six assistants and one public relations agent to look after his every need. "The poor thing's roughing it," said Karl Lagerfeld, who, like the other designers, brought no mannequins and only one assistant, though he did arrive with a Walkman wrapped around his neck and six Goyard suitcases.

Perry was peeved at Giorgio Armani, who earlier had suggested that some of his ideas had found their way into Ellis's recent collection. Armani was furious at an Italian fabric company, Etro, which last season sold Perry one of Armani's exclusive designs.

Meanwhile, Krazy Karl was trying to cope with Japanese domestic life. "I'm used to beds with canopies," he sighed. Instead, Kourageous Karl was faced with a single mattress on the tatami-matted floor. "I feel like a dachshund." In addition, he hated to take off his $2,000 Lobb shoes and eventually started hiding in his bathroom when the maid arrived so that she would not be exposed to his covered, barbarian feet. Just about his only enjoyment was filling out fake breakfast requests (fish heads, fried squid) and hanging them on Poor Perry's door.

During the day, the designers plotted their shows and tried to lure their models away from the ever-fitting Ellis. "I'm going to kill that man," cried an exasperated Maxine van Cliff, the shows' choreographer, after half of Armani's models weren't available for a rehearsal because they were trapped in Perry's *cabine*. Initially, everyone expressed disappointment in the local mannequins, but in the end almost everything came off without a hitch—save Perry's show. At the last minute he scratched all of Larry Lazlo's lighting and set arrangements and opted for bright lights that made the skipping, all-American models look like walking corpses.

The Japanese crowds, who paid $40 a head to see the fifteen shows (three for each designer), were most impressed with Armani and Lagerfeld. Only Rangy Rhodes managed to go to everyone's show (though she slept through them), and Lagerfeld went to Armani's and Ellis's. Perry went only to Lagerfeld's, although he tried to compensate by leaving "I love you" notes to everyone, including the other designers' assistants. "I was very pleased," said Pleasant Perry. "I have now been raised to the international level of Armani and Lagerfeld."

—LOUISE J. ESTERHAZY, Tokyo, 1980

At home in New York, 1984

KARL L

Karl Lagerfeld, unlike his cohorts, has made his name and earned his reputation selling his services to others: to Chloé for ready-to-wear (an eighteen-year alliance that ended in 1982), to Fendi for furs, and to dozens of lesser-known firms around the world. In 1983, after several others had tried and failed, Lagerfeld took over the design reins of Chanel couture and revitalized one of France's grandes dames.

"I'm working class, my dear," he announces often in one of the four languages he speaks at a Gatling-gun pace, usually as he's straightening the vest of his impeccable Caraceni suit or tidying the ponytail he has favored as long as anyone can remember.

Other designers are proud to have a constant identifiable look, but Lagerfeld claims his talent lies in having the right look at the right time.

His ability earns him an estimated $4 million each year, and Lagerfeld, a resident of tax-free Monaco, loves to spend it. There's a château in Brittany; a Monte Carlo apartment; and, in Paris, a pied-à-terre with the kind of exquisite Louis XV furniture for which he competes with the Louvre at auctions. "I can't say I enjoy the simple life," he admits, "but then again, we working class deserve our rewards."

AGERFELD
Conductor of the Fashion Opera

UP WITH KAISER KARL

At the moment, all that counts in the peripatetic life of fashion's most prolific designer, Karl Lagerfeld, is sketching, with the speed of light, for Chanel, Fendi, and his own two signature collections; keeping all his personal accounts for same without the help of a secretary; reading twenty history books at once; buying pop music cassettes in $500-bushel loads; consuming every newspaper and magazine in print ("I'm a paper freak," he says); out-talking left-wing radicals live on West German television, where he appears as a kind of Phil Donahue; compiling the seventeenth-century letters of Princess Palatine, about whom he is writing a book; decorating his eighteenth-century château in Brittany, a new house in Rome, and a villa perched cozily adjacent to the Royal Family of Monaco, who have adopted him as their own; and systematically donning a fresh white pique bathrobe each morning, to wipe the slate clean.

Fresh starts are what fuel fashion's most mercurial designer, provided by such rituals as changing the starched white collars on his shirts and putting scented hankies in his pockets, doused, suitably, in Calvin Klein's Obsession. ("Caroline and I are fragrance freaks," he says of the Monagasque Princess.) He has, on occasion, requested a change of bed linens in mid-nap for the pleasure of climbing back into them, and, every morning, he alters the look of the world by choosing one of his twelve pairs of tinted glasses. ("Sometimes I feel like seeing blue, sometimes pink, sometimes a more beigey color. It depends.")

Known as Kaiser Karl (the only German designer to have made it to the superstar ranks), Monte Karl (for his tax-haven homing instincts), Killer Karl ("fighting with company presidents is my favorite"), and Kitsch Karl for his addiction to pop culture, Lagerfeld is a media-mad media star who can talk—rapidly in most known languages—about anything from Sylvester Stallone to Frederick the Great and the Fine Young Cannibals, his new favorite rock group. The sole creative force behind three major fashion houses and the one who put Chanel back on the map, he is fashion's most thinly spread, but entertaining and controversial, designer, and always leaves witticisms, parody, word and war games in his wake.

"I hate fashion designers who talk too seriously about their trade. Twenty years ago they were still trade persons, let's face it. They should all be very happy that people pay them so much attention. After rock stars, and a few movie stars, it's one of the best things today, no? They make more money than everybody else," he says with characteristic commercial candor. Better than most, he understands the link between kitsch, culture, and cash, but adds, "If I wanted money for money's sake, I'd still be in canned milk"—his father was a dairy magnate.

"People find it hard to understand why one person wants to be so many different persons," he says of his role as one-man band for Fendi, Chanel, and Karl Lagerfeld. "But I know that if I would do only one thing, I would want to be suddenly somewhere else. My batteries, they get recharged from going somewhere else."

Lagerfeld talks the way he designs, like a machine gun that never needs reloading.

"You know, I talk like this because when I was a child I talked a lot. Now I am a very silent person, but then I talked a lot and my mother started to leave the room when I started a story, so I had to learn to finish the story by the time she got to the door. I must tell you, I hate people who speak very slowly. I fall asleep. There is no reason to bore people with one little story for half an hour.

"I don't believe in stops," he continues. "Fashion is change. To be in it you have to be a kind of intellectual opportunist, which I think is a very healthy attitude. I'm bored by designers who have one style and never want to move from that, because the interesting thing about fashion is that it reflects, over a very short period, the spirit of the moment."

The moment, for Lagerfeld, is music. "Music is the most important fashion influence, if you ask me, more important than movies, or anything. It's like fashion: it has to be the latest of the latest," he says. He's known for bringing traffic to a halt at Paris's Champs Disc, his favorite music store, when he buys 300 tapes at a time. "I buy everything, keep them, file them. My collection is going to be a very important document because who buys so many?" Having heralded Madonna to the point where all the girls in the Chanel studio now dress like her, Lagerfeld now cites Sade, the cool jazz singer, as his rock muse, and her photograph is already tacked up on the Chanel studio wall as inspiration.

In décor, however, his taste inclines to the traditional. "I prefer the eighteenth century for taste and look. But for history, the seventeenth century is much more interesting," he explains. And he has not diverged "one centimeter" from his addiction to eighteenth-century furnishings since the age of four.

Lagerfeld describes his upbringing during wartime as that of an only child left to his imaginative devices in the bleak countryside of northern Germany. "I never played with other children. I read books and did drawings night and day. At five, I started my French lessons with a teacher who was one of the fifty-six war refugees who lived in our country castle outside Hamburg after World War II. I made early preparations for coming to France," he explains.

"I had this feeling," he continues, "that my parents had lived fabulous lives between the wars and that I had been

Fendi, 1981

Chloé, 1979

Lagerfeld,
1986

Lagerfeld,
1987

Lagerfeld,
1986

Chloé,
1980

born too late in a lousy period." (His mother, his lasting model of sartorial sophistication, maintained that women should not wear shiny gems beyond a certain age except on their ears. " 'The ears don't age,' she used to say.")

And while he hoards cultural and historical documents, Lagerfeld's great gift is his obliviousness to anything but the here-and-now. "I keep nothing of my work, no sketches, no photos, nothing." And the more he discards, the more he can produce.

"I am so bored by designers who think their style is too important to be changed and who think life was so much better in Paris ten years ago, and fashion was so much more elegant. Who cares? They should find out why they're not having an interesting time now," he says with characteristic adamance.

Since he launched himself into the limelight at the time of Yves Saint Laurent's emergence in the early Sixties,

many of Lagerfeld's latter-day railings sound like veiled criticisms of the Parisian haute artistes—YSL included. Like his Monte Carlo "home without a past" as he calls the skyscraper apartment of which he has now tired, Lagerfeld is a superstar in isolation, a phenomenon of internationalism who lives at a deliberate remove from old, local allegiances. His sixteen-year relationship with the house of Chloé, where he built his career, ended bitterly in 1983, and while

"But I must admit, what I've done isn't all that bad."

Fendi, 1981

Chloé, 1980

Lagerfeld, 1984

Lagerfeld, 1985

Lagerfeld, 1987

Lagerfeld, 1985

he is godfather to the son of Anne Marie Munoz, top assistant at Yves Saint Laurent, his once-close friendship with the designer and his business partner, Pierre Bergé, has turned to stony rivalry.

"It isn't modern to be attached to a city," he says. He has never voted in any country and is appalled by national French politics. ("They fight like prostitutes.") "I prefer the monarchic principle," he adds of life in Monaco. "Then you don't have to discuss such things and

it's more fun, no?"

For some. Thanks to his cozy rapport with the Grimaldis, he will soon move into prime cliff-hanging real estate—a refurbished villa perched safe and sound, he likes to note, above the Palace. "It's the safest place in the world. You can't walk on the street or stop a car. It's like a police state, but today I think it's a good idea, no?" Owned by the principality's Société de Bains Mers, it will function as a museum and

reception hall downstairs, with Monte Karl its resident "curator" upstairs. "I like Monte Carlo because it's a tiny Manhattan with no provincial touches. It really feels like home," he adds.

But more than any of his houses, home for Lagerfeld is the design studios (one in Rome, two in Paris, and one in New York), the staffs of which function, he admits, "like my family."

"They are all friends, kids, cousins, nephews of people I've known for years," he says of the gangs of devotees, who at Chanel include his right-hand man of twenty years, Gilles du Four; muse number one, Ines de la Fressange; muse number two, Victoire de Castellane, du Four's niece; and a harem of little Madonnas, as in the rock star. "I think it's a very healthy atmosphere because, with all my businesses functioning as licensing arrangements (there are about fifty, stretching to Japan and the United States and covering everything from sunglasses to porcelain tableware), none of them are my employees. That I would hate."

In Rome, the five Fendi sisters embrace him as their prodigal son, and nowhere is he so fawned over by the general public as in West Germany. Swarms of German tourists have been known to engulf him outside the casino in Monaco, waving their note pads for his autograph.

"But it's not because I'm the only German designer ever to be known in the rest of the world," he says, attributing his native popularity instead to the curiosity he creates as a West German TV talk show host. "Germans aren't used to my machine-gun answers," he says of the dumbfounding verbal volleys he deals his guests, whom he describes as "all sorts, lots of crazies, mean ones and nice ones but I like the mean ones better." He sees none of them until show time, and he insists on performing live because "that way I can say anything I want"—including plugging his products.

While he claims to hate seeking money for its own sake, Lagerfeld remain's fashion's shrewdest businessman, a self-sufficient public relations master

who involves himself in every detail of image making. "I will never forgive Miss D'Alessio for the story of the blue glove," he says of the Chanel president's decision, against his advice, to "stick an old stuffed blue glove on Ines's forehead" in an ad campaign.

"I think I'm the easiest person to work with as long as things are the way I think they should be. And normally everybody makes quite a lot of money by doing what I think they should and some of them made a name and fortune, so nobody can cry. I don't cry either," he says.

Self-mockery, timed to cut the bite of a diatribe, is Lagerfeld's forte, second only to word games. A former bodybuilder—he loves Arnold Schwarzenegger—Lagerfeld once tried acupuncture in the back of the knee to cure a sweet tooth, swears by a scalp masseuse who cured his receding hairline, and has only recently stopped powdering the pony-tailed coif he has been wearing as long as anyone can remember because "now that I'm gray it looks like an old oxtail."

"I'm born to be a vieux garçon," he says. "If I were a woman, I'd probably have a dozen children. But as I'm a man, I'd rather buy a dog," he muses, citing Ines de la Fressange, Tina Chow, and Princess Caroline as his aesthetic ideals of femininity. Believing that "la femme" makes a house come alive, he has enlisted his great friend and decorator, Sabine Imbert, to coordinate all his domestic décors. Now, with ten years' work on restoring the gardens of his Brittany château complete, she has moved into a neighboring house to begin four more years of assembling its interior. In Rome, he has just finished creating "a northern house under a southern sky."

"I'm not from Middle Europe. I am a Northerner. That's why I had to get rid of all my late-nineteenth-century stuff. I did not get good vibrations, it was too decadent. The eighteenth century is fresh with lots of energy and a kind of mental health," he concludes. But as always, the completion of one Lagerfeld project marks the launching of others, from the sublime to the most improbable.

He recently decided that his chauffeur-driven vehicle of choice would be a customized, luxury-lined Volkswagen bus, replete with videos and airline seats. Why? "Because I don't like to travel so low to the ground," he explains. —PARIS, 1986

"I think I'm the easiest person to work with as long as things are the way I think they should be. And normally everybody makes quite a lot of money by doing what I think they should and some of them made a name and fortune, so nobody can cry. I don't cry either."

Working out at home

KL ON HOW A MAN SHOULD DRESS

A man should dress by instinct: His wardrobe should match his life, looks, and personality. For me, shirts are the basis of everything. I love them very well made and perfectly pressed. I only let one cleaner press my shirts, and I'd never send them out when I'm at a hotel.

"I don't like suits; they make me feel too businesslike. I prefer pants and jackets, things you can mix your own way.

"Accessories have to be very refined—impeccable and of great quality—like nice cuff links and a money clip.

"I'm mad for beautiful shoes and they must be well maintained, kept on a mold and polished. Classic shoes in black and brown can look beautiful, but at times I like different colors—like the olive green used in old luggage and the interiors of old cars. Bright colors are good for sweaters, ties, and waistcoats.

"For evening wear, you must have good quality. I love white piqué waistcoats and starched shirts. I don't like patent leather for shoes because it's all plastic now. Glove leather is better, especially when it's shiny and well kept. Evening stockings should always be silk with no design. The worst thing is to see a man in evening wear with ribbed socks.

"I like marvelous pajamas and matching robes in white material like piqué. I have mine washed daily. There's nothing more revolting than a not-too-well-groomed man over thirty-five."

1985

1984

1985

1985

1986

A man who seems perpetually in transit, Karl Lagerfeld can pull off a sketch for a new design in the time it takes most people to unwrap a stick of gum. He delivered his own best self-portrait shortly after he picked up the designing reins at Chanel. "I'm like a computer," he said, "who for the moment is plugged in at the House of Chanel."

1984

1986

KL'S CHANEL

I t's a challenge to do couture in a modern way. And I like challenge," said Karl Lagerfeld when he took over the designing duties at Chanel, beginning with the January 1983 collection. "The body of the Eighties is very different from the body of the Fifties. Today's woman has lots of shoulders, a long waist, hips that are not round, and long, long legs. Changes in fashion come from change in movement, in attitude."

Accordingly, in Lagerfeld's incarnation of the eternally lucrative Chanel suit fussy details were eliminated in favor of scaled-up proportions and cleaner, more supple lines. Buttons were bigger, the multiplicity of waist and neck-strung chains was eliminated in favor of the larger single chain, and the traditional Chanel braid vanished almost completely.

In subsequent seasons Lagerfeld has felt his way with an increasingly sure hand toward a satisfactory compromise between his own freewheeling imagination and Chanel's strict classicism. By the spring '85 collection he had created the kickiest, most modern-looking, and sexiest Chanel in years, while still retaining that identifiable Chanel imprimatur. The eternal question remains: Would Coco have liked it? Probably not, but on the other hand, she probably stopped turning in her grave.

The Launching of a Fragrance

There is about to be a party to mark the European launch of Karl Lagerfeld's KL perfume, but the designer isn't very excited. "I'll have to work up some passion," he groans. "These are not the days for parties."

But that's Karl Lagerfeld when he's pondering the state of the nation. His saving grace is that he doesn't do it too often or for too long. A few hours later, in fact, after a healthy portion of sushi at his favorite Japanese restaurant, the designer's spirits are lifted, and although he isn't quite ready to admit that he loves organizing big bashes, he does acknowledge that the KL launch holds more than a passing interest. Lagerfeld and a team from Elizabeth Arden worked on the fragrance for two years, and the resulting scent "is really not bad at all," he suggests.

"We found that a lot of women were using the Lagerfeld men's fragrance, and this is a feminine version for them. KL is spicier and fruitier than Chloé, perhaps even a little lighter. If pushed, I would say it's for a woman with an active life, who wants to wear perfume and wants the world to know she wears perfume, but doesn't want to hit anybody over the head."

Lagerfeld has to be "pushed" because he believes "fragrances shouldn't be compared—it's impossible to tell one woman she should use Chloé or Chanel No. 5 or L'Air du Temps and then tell another she should wear KL or whatever else she can buy. Scent isn't like a bottle of medicine. It's all about fantasy and each woman has to make her own."

As a true devotee of the eighteenth century, Lagerfeld prefers heavy fragrances for himself as well as his homes. Asked to list his favorites, he names powerful ones like Caron's Narcisse Noir or the scents Guerlain made in the Twenties. He likes perfumes that linger in the air after a lady withdraws. "As long as the smell is pleasant, I find that leftover scent is the most exotic sensation in the world. It is the definition of luxury."

KL is Lagerfeld's third perfume, following Chloé (1975) and Lagerfeld for men (1978). The new fragrance was to be called Fanatic, after the designer's well-known passion for fans, but there were copyright problems, and at the last minute Lagerfeld and Arden were forced to change the name and abandon the expensive promotional campaign they had developed around the theme.

"KL wasn't anyone's first choice for another name," says the designer, "but we had to come up with something—and quick." Arden, however, has kept the original fan-shaped crystal bottle and the gray fanlike plastic covering. And to mark the perfume's European launch, the company is publishing a deluxe edition of the history of the fan that Lagerfeld and a friend put together.

Unlike some other designers, Lagerfeld doesn't like to make "serious statements" about his perfumes. He claims to be embarrassed by the Chloé advertising motto—"A woman doesn't wear my perfume, she enters it"—because it smacks of "intellectualism."

"I may like heavy scents," says Lagerfeld, "but I don't like heavy pronouncements. They make me weary."

—PARIS, 1982

Jacqueline de Ribes in ponytail and YSL

The menu

CASTING A BALLET

When Karl Lagerfeld threw the first big social event of the Paris fall season it was, as expected, a no-expense-barred evening. With indefatigable co-host Ira von Furstenberg at his side, Lagerfeld opened his home to 100 select guests, including a host of Paris party regulars and a visiting Barbara Walters. The occasion: a sit-down dinner after the New York City Ballet premiere at the Théâtre des Champs-Élysées to benefit the Foundation for Medical Research.

An hour before dinner, Lagerfeld and his guests were at the ballet, clapping solidly for Mikhail Baryshnikov and Peter Martins. Meanwhile, back at

The fan-shaped KL bottle

Mikhail Baryshnikov and Princess Caroline in Dior

Charlotte Aillaud, Jean Marie Riviere, and Hélène Rochas

The host with Marie-Hélène de Rothschild

Andrée Putman in Chloé

The Lagerfeld-designed fruit and vegetable chandelier

the house, where a staff of seventy-five had been hired for the event, a mild sort of hysteria was in swing as tuxedoed waiters rushed about slipping rolls onto plates and candles into candelabra. Chairs were arranged around several dozen oval tables spread throughout the main salon, secondary salon, and dining room.

The kitchen—usually a spic-and-span study in modern black and white—had been drastically transformed: Le Nôtre, which catered the dinner, had shipped in five massive metal ice-boxes, extra electrical generators, bolts of rubber matting to cover the floor tile, and ten huge blocks of white marble on which to prepare the dinner.

Even Lagerfeld's mini-gym had been turned into a storage area for the 100 bottles of pink Piper-Heidsieck Champagne, 50 bottles of whiskey, and 100 bottles of red and white wine, which had been consumed by the time the last

guests left at 3 A.M.

By 11, the waiters had taken their places at the tables, and the crowds crossed Lagerfeld's stone-paved court-yard unhampered by photographers. Christiana Brandolini was one of the first to arrive—and depart, as she had somehow forgotten to inform her host that she was bringing three friends, who could not be seated due to lack of space. Clad in electric blue, Marie-Hélène de Rothschild breezed in and pronounced the house "exquisite," as did a pony-tailed Jacqueline de Ribes.

Dinner was "light," as the host described it, and "intelligently satisfying," as guest Gilles Dufour put it. To start, there was a "pyramid" of foie gras, its presentation unforgettable—large oval silver platters with staircase structures of foie gras leading up to baskets holding real (but deceased) mallard ducks with their wings propped up and their necks at the proper arch. After the foie gras

came young chicken in a light cream sauce with wild mushrooms, rice pilaf, a chocolate and meringue cake, and finally an eye-opener of vodka sherbet, chosen because Baryshnikov supposedly is fond of strong desserts.

As after-dinner drinks were served the harpsichord and flute started up again, and Princess Caroline was suddenly in the middle of a group of dancers including Martins (whose entrance had drawn applause), Patricia McBride, and Heather Watts.

At 2:30, most of the older group were on their way out. And at 3, von Furstenberg, Lagerfeld, and Princess Caroline headed for Castel's, leaving behind only the seventy-five servants to clean up. "When you entertain like this it doesn't make sense to invite less than a hundred people," said Lagerfeld. "I think I should do this more often—it's a nice way to spend an evening."

—PARIS, 1979

KARL LAGERFELD 97

THE BED BUG

For Karl Lagerfeld, the idea of a bed is tantamount to his extraordinary lifestyle: He reads, recuperates, sleeps, dreams, "and yes, daydreams" on any of the five beds in his Rue de l'Université home. "Beds are one of the most important things in my life. I love big beds, and daybeds which are like beds. In my Paris home there is a bed in every room except the dining room," he says, surveying the massive eighteenth-century masterpiece—a lit de parade (state bed)—that dominates the main salon. "People would be all dressed up lying on top of the cover while people came in and conversed or listened to music," he explains. The bed is covered by a cream silk spread heavily encrusted with gold thread, galloons, passementerie, and pearl beads. Each corner of the spread depicts one of the four seasons. "When I have people in, they really don't sit on it. I suppose they're a bit afraid of the splendor of it."

His guests often end up on the other beds, however, including one guest room's Louis XVI bed covered with striped silk faille and the daybed, de-signed by Cressant, in Lagerfeld's work-room. "I like life on beds," he explains, shrugging. "Even as a child I felt the importance of beds. All I need in life is a comfortable bed and a desk to work at."

Lagerfeld's bed philosophy is in keeping with the ambience of his Parisian home. Although the apartment receives a considerable amount of natural light by day, at night the light in all the rooms except bedrooms (which have lamps) is derived from candles, an effect that makes it as romantic as if it were another century. The idea of working on a satin-covered daybed by candlelight is very Lagerfeld.

"My beds are not necessarily stationary objects," he explains. "Any of these beds can be moved from corner to corner, wall to wall, room to room. That

Lagerfeld on the *lit de parade* (state bed) in his formal Four Seasons room. In the eighteenth century, such a bed was used for receiving guests. He is wearing an eighteenth-century coral and fern-green silk Chinese robe edged in ermine.

OF PARIS

appeals to me. One should be able to create one's preferred atmosphere at any moment. If I feel I would like very much to have my big eighteenth-century bed in the foyer, then I move it there—pure and simple.'' —PARIS, 1979

The guest room's Louis XVI bed in striped silk faille

Heurteaut's matching brocade bed and chair, in Lagerfeld's bedroom

In Lagerfeld's workroom, the daybed designed by Cressant

Road Show

I n New York for the first stop in a four-city tour to promote his KL fragrance in America, Karl Lagerfeld is returning from an 8 A.M. meeting with Elizabeth Arden. He enters the lobby of the Hotel Pierre looking like an impeccably dressed, well-heeled European in his custom-made (Caraceni, of course) houndstooth jacket. The only difference is that he is wearing his signature ponytail and carrying a fan.

He is also wearing three small tiepins, two in the shape of a cloverleaf and the other a horseshoe. "One never has enough luck," he says, also mentioning the more common "you can't be too rich or too thin" counterpart. Lagerfeld is certainly thinner, having lost about thirty pounds on an acupuncture diet. Rich? "It depends on the budget of the person asking."

Since his arrival three days ago, Lagerfeld has stood in the rain at Saks Fifth Avenue to look at his embroidered evening dresses in the store's windows, seen the art exhibit of the Mexican painter Frida Kahlo, and bought two hats at Jay Lord Hatters—a dark brown one to wear in the wind and rain at home in Brittany and a straw Panama to wear at home in Monte Carlo. He also stopped

Lagerfeld's Monte Carlo panama straw hat

at Barney's to buy a private-label raincoat and a French-made umbrella. Saturday night he went to Tina Chow's birthday party—"everyone was from London and Paris"—and Sunday afternoon he took his goddaughters (the adopted Vietnamese daughters of Jacqueline and Yul Brynner) to Central Park.

Being in the U.S., he says, is fun because it is not what he usually does, but he makes it clear that "what I enjoy

about my job is the job." Holidays he considers boring. "Traveling on business is what life is all about," says Lagerfeld, who spends four days of any given week on the road.

"What I like about places is that they are all different from each other." Except for his native Germany. "Germany is like America, and I don't like copies." As a resident of Monaco, Lagerfeld is not concerned about the French government's restriction on holiday travel. "It's like being behind the Iron Curtain." Yet he claims he was never interested in politics, saying, "I am too much into fashion, and fashion is based on change."

Lagerfeld finds fashion mavericks interesting from a philosophical point of view. "It's very good to have some wolves in with the sheep. If you see something different, you ask yourself questions. If things become too routine you don't look at your own things the way you should look at them."

As for himself, Lagerfeld insists that he never thinks about what he is doing, but rather works by instinct. But instinct must be trained, like practicing the piano, he says.

He says he tries to forget his collections because "people who remember what they did before tend to do the same thing over again." And he dislikes designers who say " 'I did that five years ago.' Perhaps they did, but who cares, if it wasn't the right moment? Fashion is a kind of healthy opportunism."

A new style must follow fashion; it has to evolve. A twenty-year-old suit, he notes, looks like a twenty-year-old suit. "Nobody can escape fashion. The fashion of no fashion is still fashion. People who refuse fashion get it as a markdown later anyway."

The most important thing for Lagerfeld is "never to compare, never to compete, except with yourself. Don't do things because others are doing it. Do it because you think you should do it." The unpardonable sin is to be blasé, "to think you have seen it all, done it all—it's the worst attitude."

Then he rises to try on his new hats, changing from his houndstooth jacket into a cream wool flannel for the straw Panama. "When I was a child I never went without a hat," he says as he adjusts the brim. He stands back for an inspection and adds, "I was overdressed to death."

—NEW YORK, 1983

The key to feeling at ease in any country is always to be neat, clean, and unslovenly-looking,'' says Karl Lagerfeld, who travels to airports with two cars—one for himself and companions and another for the luggage.

"Fashion is a game with no rules—and at the same time, you have to know all the rules. There's a last-minute element in fashion that you can't predict, and that's why I like it."

Chloé, 1980

Gianfranco Ferre came to fashion by way of architecture, and he has never stopped striving for the perfect master plan. He is the design intellectual of Milan's big-gun talents, and his clothes take the form of an elegantly balanced composition, leavened by the humor and good-naturedness that mark the man. He has taken inspiration from such varied themes as musketeers and mirror-image games played in double-jacketed suits. But however complex his designs may be in the making, they fall in the fluid lines that Ferre holds as key to his ideal of clean comfort. In a fashion capital not known for its facility with evening wear, Ferre is heralded as a Milanese master of the entrance-maker, which makes its presence known through understatement. His name appears on ready-to-wear, a signature fragrance, and a couture collection introduced in July 1986.

GIANFRANCO
Milan's Architect of Fashion

FERRE

Pitch pine deck chairs

There were more than a few frustrating moments when Gianfranco Ferre thought it would have been easier to have built his vacation house from scratch. But love knows no reason, and when the architect-turned-fashion-designer first set eyes on the eighteenth-century villa overlooking Lake Maggiore, about fifty miles north of his home in Milan, he knew he had to have it. Never mind that it was a desolate, uninhabitable shambles, or that—because of the house's historical-landmark status—every detail of reconstruction had to be approved by a local board of officials.

"I couldn't even paint it without getting permission to use the color I'd chosen," says Ferre, as he surveys the object of over four years of labor from his sloping front lawn. He casts a glowering look at the statues topping the villa's roof, which are the reason for the house's inclusion on Italy's map of historical buildings. "The four seasons, as usual." He yawns, rolling his eyes.

It may have taken four years of aggravation before he was ready to move in, but Ferre says now he's realized exactly the flavor he'd hoped to achieve in a weekend home. "I knew I didn't want a 'fashion' house," says Ferre, who, after all, has to live with fashion most of the year. He says he deliberately set out to create a neutral atmosphere reflecting

Lunch from Mama Ferre

A terrace view of Lake Maggiore

"no particular style—just a mixture of paintings and objects I love, and colors I find absolutely relaxing."

By the standards of the second homes maintained by the Milanese fashion community, Ferre's house is not extreme, falling somewhere between the stark minimalism of Giorgio Armani's Pantelleria beach compound and the baroque splendor of Gianni Versace's palatial Como retreat. Ferre's house exudes a calming quality of understatement, reflected most conspicuously in soothing colors—a mélange of creams, corals, peach, and white; the mixture of modern and antique furniture, and the calculated throwaway effect of drawings by Picasso and Modigliani propped casu-

FERRE'S TRANQUIL RETREAT

Looking out from the dining room

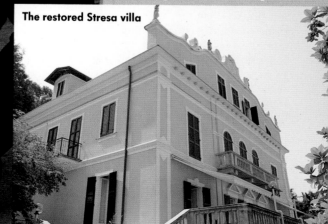

The restored Stresa villa

An Oriental-flavored table setting in the glassed-in dining room

ally against the walls in corners.

Ferre's evenhanded eclecticism is very much in evidence in the central living room, where quintessentially Milanese low sofas and ottomans are grouped conversationally next to a leather camp bed copied from an eighteenth-century original in Ferre's grandmother's house. Then there is the juxtaposition of cool, Lombardy-style sealed cement walls and copper track lighting. Discreetly but meticulously arranged on clean wood surfaces are antique maritime equipment, including two beautiful nineteenth-century English telescopes, and lacquered boxes from Russia, India, and China. A gallery of framed madonnas hangs in a guest bedroom.

The ten bedrooms are cozily small and deliberately utilitarian, with low ceilings and walls of white pine. If there is a marked absence of strong color in these rooms, it is because Ferre has chosen not to compete with the rich spectrum of shades surrounding the hazy, mountain-framed lake or with his azalea-and-rhododendron-filled gardens. In fact, whenever possible he brings a sense of the vibrant landscape into the house—in the French windows of the living room which open onto the lakeview terrace or in the glassed-in dining room, an ingenious arrangement of windows and mirrors that gives the feeling

Ferre in his thoroughly modern kitchen

of openness.

In this lushly pastoral setting, Ferre says, he finds a serenity he could never hope for in Milan. "It's completely another world. There's no one in front of you, no one behind you, no one to look at you." When he's in Stresa he tries to do as little as possible, "to make a very normal life," a pursuit that includes reading, talking quietly with visiting family and friends, and taking his two-motor eleven-meter boat out onto the lake.

And then there is the good Piedmontese-style food, the consumption of which is one of gourmand Gianfranco's favorite pastimes. Like all good Italian

sons, Ferre says that his mother, Andreina, who lives in nearby Legnano, is the best cook he knows. On this particular day she has sent over a summer lunch of cold small veal scallops, chicken salad, melon and prosciutto, rolled veal and vegetables, and, for dessert, three flavors of homemade gelato—a repast Ferre says represents just the kind of light, simple fare he loves in hot weather.

Since Ferre realizes that such special catering service is not to be expected every day even from the most devoted mother, he's having his own cook, a cheerful young woman named Maria Felice, take a few lessons from Mama. "She's giving Maria her cooking secrets," says Ferre, "but one by one."

Perhaps by the time Maria has acquired the complete Mama Ferre cookbook Ferre will have completed all the improvements he has planned for his five-acre Stresa estate. He points out where he wants a swimming pool, and indicates a greenhouse that he plans to convert into a guesthouse. This greenhouse is the sort of collapsing roofless structure that could make the ruins of Rome look whole in comparison. Nevertheless, Ferre, having tackled and mastered a wholly decrepit old villa, is sure he can make something out of it.

—STRESA, ITALY, 1984

The style of Milanese designer Gianfranco Ferre and the technique behind it are unique; it is usually sophisticated, sleek, painstakingly constructed, deceptively simple—some say "intellectual"—and never, ever, frilly. American buyers alternately have classified Ferre as "extremely chic," "hard to understand," "smartly cerebral," and finally, based on his performance in stores, extremely salable.

This designer, who was formally trained as an architect, is a bit of an oddball in a city where designers have made their reputations on classic jackets, sensibly kicky sportswear, and understated evening clothes. Since his company opened in 1978 Ferre's style has been based essentially on architecturally constructed shapes, clear or somber colors, and a good deal of complicated details. Ferre started in the fashion business as a busy, anonymous free-lance designer and has become a name that stands up to the likes of Giorgio Armani and Gianni Versace. He credits his "swift" stardom to his technique, which appears to be like no one else's.

Like other fashion makers', Ferre's collections start the minute the last collection clears the runway. He usually takes a two- to three-week vacation then—"always, always, always by the sea, because the mountains don't interest me"—and it is between sunburns and long leisurely meals that Ferre's colors and themes jell. "Everything is, of course, a bit vague in the beginning," he

HIGH STYLE AND HIGH TECH

1981

"What does fashion mean to me? To be conscious of woman herself...to be simple...to be clean...to love white all year round...to love soft cashmere...to love very simple gold watches."

1985

1984

1982

1985

1983

1987

1985

1984

1982

1983

1987

1985

1986

says. "I usually start with the type of fabric that will be the cornerstone of the collection. Sometimes I feel like smooth silk or sometimes plush wools. The fabric calls the construction shots."

After Ferre has about three hundred sketches, full-figure and partial, he edits them and selects the ideas that will be given to one of the several companies that produce his clothes. His drawings are a far cry from romantic portraits of stylish women: One can easily see his training as a designer of buildings in the sure, rounded, and graphic lines of his drawings. He uses large colored markers for accents, and sometimes adds a sketch of a belt or a hat in a corner of the page. Unlike many designers, Ferre does his fittings in the fabric in which the dress or pants or suit will eventually be made. He has never touched a toile, and doesn't like "the idea of fitting a dress in stiff

toile when it will actually be fabricated in a luxurious cashmere or a soft knit. It simply doesn't work."

Since many of his cuts are unusual, a good deal of trial and error goes into the making of a collection. He says he will try three times to get something right, and only then will he "throw in the towel." His leather clothes are a good example of his inventiveness: He treats leather as though it were not a stiff fabric, sometimes loading a jacket with as many as several dozen quilted, welted, curved seams.

After the prototypes are made (all of which have been fitted personally by Ferre), groups are planned. Again unlike most designers, Ferre gets his collection together by category. He starts, for example, with skirts, looking at the ten or thirty skirt designs and deciding which should be done away with and which themes should be supplemented. He does the same thing with blouses. Then pants. Then suits. Then dresses. Then coats. And, finally, evening clothes. The whole thing crystallizes at the last minute.

In the interim, Ferre fits complicated belts and details on an amusing miniature dress dummy, about a foot high, which he keeps on a cluttered worktable next to his desk. This season, the little dummy was girdled with mini-versions of the stiff and large obi belts he was preparing for the fall collection. As he fits the belts, he draws them. Then he fits again; then he draws more. It is a fairly exhausting process to watch.

HE TOLD W

The look of my collection has been changing—it's simpler, less architectural. But to get to this point, I had to go through those other collections. Season after season I have been trying to trim the excess, to take away. Now there's a simpler mood. The shapes are very simple. There are no pleats. Jackets are shaped with a subtle vertical line . . . no gimmicks. It's an evolution to the cleanest shapes.

"That was the kind of approach people had in ancient times. That's why I'm thinking about the Orient now, particularly China and India. They're older than Europe, and I like the energy that comes out of the Eastern cultures.

"I am using those influences in this collection. Things that are simple but with energy—like wrapping a soft jersey belt high on the waist. It has a different attitude." —MILAN, 1985

Beyond the great fitting techniques, the miniature dummy, the drawings that look like blueprints, and his refreshingly timid character, perhaps the thing that makes Ferre a special case is his view of "the ideal customer." Ask designers about their archetypal client and nine out of ten will say such things as "an attractive woman who has a certain style," or "a young woman who knows what's going on and wants to be attractive," or "someone who has enormous chic." Ferre's response: "Beauty has nothing to do with it. I hardly ever think of my ideal customer as particularly beautiful. But she must have one very important thing—intelligence. Pure and simple. Intelligence."   —MILAN, 1981

1984

"I believe in the blazer," said a youthful Ralph Lauren, the only major American designer to make his entrée into women's wear through men's wear, in 1971. Now in his mid-forties, the designer has remained true to his tenet, having cut the classic jacket in everything from tartan wools to silk tweeds, often playing it against luxuriously feminine fabrics.

If his seemingly unorthodox style is not in tune with the prevailing mood— "I don't want to be part of any trend," he has maintained over the years—it is nevertheless his own, a style by turns rugged and romantic, inspired by American folklore, English aristocracy, and Ivy League prep. The formula has served him well—in home furnishings as well as men's, women's, and children's fashions, all of which are now showcased in Manhattan's historic Rhinelander mansion, restored by Lauren to become his flagship Polo/Ralph Lauren store.

Success has enabled the Urban Cowboy to live the life of the real thing on a huge Colorado spread. And when, like his fashions, he makes the switch to a more sophisticated style, there's the Montego Bay getaway; the Montauk beach house; the ten-room duplex on Fifth Avenue that serves as home base; plus 115 acres in nearby Pound Ridge.

RALPH

LAUREN
America's Preppy Cowboy

Lauren in one of his vintage vehicles

HOME ON THE RANGE

It's 1:30 on a Friday afternoon and Ralph Lauren is sitting in his Hawker Siddeley jet about 35,000 feet over Ohio. Uncommonly relaxed, he is nibbling a tuna fish sandwich and talking about his life.

"Ever since I can remember I've thought about style," he says. "When I was a kid I didn't think about buying Cadillacs or big motorcycles, but I did think about woody station wagons." To young Ralph, those station wagons symbolized a whole world of Ivy League-ish comfort and tradition. They had an ease and sturdiness he admired. "I dreamed about owning one and everything that went with it."

The West also played a role in Lauren's style-conscious dreams. "I believed the myth, if it was a myth," he says. "When I watched the movies or read the books I only saw the purity of the West. It wasn't plastic like so much of America. It had true character, as much as anything in England. It was old. I wanted to move there, and one day I knew I would."

And so he has. On this very afternoon, Lauren and his two pilots are headed toward what could be described as a self-constructed fantasy land: a 10,000-acre ranch deep in the mountains of southern Colorado where Lauren has fashioned, piece by authentic piece, his vision of the Western good life.

The ranch is called the Double RL, named for Ralph and his wife, Ricky, and it stretches, trite though it might sound, as far as the eye can see. "I feel small, minute here," observes Lauren, and anybody would. The edge of the property, which Lauren bought in 1981, is guarded by the snow-capped San Juan Mountains, an extension of the Rockies. They loom behind every view and provide a magnificent, movie-set backdrop for the thousands of acres of aspen forest, sage gullies, and faded green pastures.

Lauren searched long and hard for his ranch, and at various times, while shopping with his friends Tom McGuane and Robert Redford, almost chose spreads in Wyoming and Utah. But he finally settled on Colorado because of the landscape and the state's long seasons. "I always look for a 'Wow!' in things and this place screams 'Wow!'" explains the forty-six-year-old designer. "This is not some little ranch. It's a knockout. There's a natural extravagance here that I find irresistible."

Lauren also liked the spread because it was virtually empty, and he could freely create his ideal ranch—part Zane Grey, part Ralph Lauren, the fashion and home furnishings designer. He has spent millions building roads, digging ponds, clearing pastures, and mending stables. He has also decided to enclose the entire property in a pristine white fence. There's already 15 miles of it and Lauren seems undaunted by the prospect that the task will take another four or five years.

"I want everything to be real," he insists, and when Lauren built several houses on the property he used only antique wood, much of it dating from the mid-nineteenth century, which he bought from dealers or took from ramshackle cabins on his own land. The furnishings are equally, painstakingly, genuine, from the skins of mountain lions and raccoons on the walls to the Indian rugs on the floors and creaking screens on the doors. Lauren has left

> "I believed the myth, if it was a myth. When I watched the movies or read the books I only saw the purity of the West. I wanted to move there, and one day I knew I would."

nothing to chance. Even with modern necessities, like lighting and plumbing, the designer was careful to bring in experts who could make them as unobtrusive as possible.

The ranch consists of a series of dispersed dwellings. The Laurens and their three children stay in what's called the Lodge, a spacious, two-story house with high, beamed ceilings, enormous hearths, and the open, expansive feel of a meticulously planned building. In fact, the house was built twice. After it was constructed the first time, Lauren decided it didn't look right and he ordered the frame dismantled and rebuilt. A mile or so away is the guest cabin, known as the Cottage, which has two bedrooms, a small kitchen, and a sitting room, and overlooks a brook and the ranch's corral.

Between the Lodge and the Cottage are the stables and the Cookhouse. With its wooden plank floors, soft glowing lanterns, and photographs of the Old West by Edward Curtis and William Henry Jackson, the Cookhouse is Lauren's pride and joy. It's where he often entertains guests, meets with his ranch manager, Larry Luke, and where he and his six ranch hands get together for breakfast. In the Cookhouse, Lauren makes sure there is always a blazing fire and good solid American food, served up by Dee, the ranch's amiable cook.

Breakfast talk is about rodeos and rustling. But the Double RL is also a working ranch, with 1,600 head of cattle, and Luke, who lives on the property, is full of news about an artificial insemination program and Lauren's plan to produce first-rate beef.

"I want the ranch to earn its own way eventually," says Lauren. He and Luke have started raising cattle without benefit of chemicals or hormones, and one day, Lauren suggests, select supermarkets across America could be selling Lauren beef. "I know about marketing, and this can be marketed," says the designer, who, like ranchers everywhere, also knows that thick juicy steaks are no longer fashionable. Even Lauren's doctor has recommended that he eat beef as seldom as possible, but Lauren believes that with the right packaging and promotion, "the idea can work."

Lauren also says he would like to raise horses and perhaps build a resort on a favorite slope high in the mountains. "Not a *resort* resort," he explains, "but something quiet and discreet. Just a few houses that can't see each other, and maybe a communal cookhouse. A lot of people want what I want—to be here."

In fact, Lauren doesn't spend all that much time at the Double RL. He only manages to make the four-hour trip to Colorado on occasional weekends and at Thanksgiving and Easter. He and his family also try to spend one month here each summer.

Every so often, Lauren considers moving full time to Colorado. "I don't really like all that New York stuff," he says. "Who are you sitting next to at the museum dinner? Are you at the right table in a restaurant? Are you being recognized? There aren't any of those kinds of pressures on a ranch. And there are days I think I could run things from here. But then I realize that if I did that it wouldn't be a place to escape to any more."

Lauren's days at the ranch usually begin at 7 A.M. with jogging and a dunk in the pool, and the Jacuzzi, next to the

Out on the range

The entrance to the Double RL

of his own brand of Stetsons. He even has his chaps tailored so they fit precisely. He prefers to drive beat-up trucks and jeeps and has a score of vintage vehicles lined up outside the Lodge. They include a wonderful 1936 Ford pickup that Lauren saw a cowboy driving down Ridgway's main street one day. Without much hesitation, the designer followed the truck home and offered the stunned driver a price he couldn't refuse.

Details like that matter to Lauren, matter a great deal, and when he talks about his past he often employs them to explain his emotions. He remembers, for instance, that when he was growing up in the Bronx, most of his friends wore leather jackets and tight pants while he preferred tweeds or bermudas and white bucks. "These clothes represented glamor to me," he says. "I wanted them, not to pretend to be somebody else, but because I found them beautiful."

His understanding that millions of other Americans shared similar desires prompted the creation of a fashion business that is today one of the world's most successful. His company, Polo Fashions, Inc. (of which he owns 90 percent), has a wholesale volume of $600 million, most of it derived from its 22 licensees, and Lauren's income is said to exceed $15 million a year.

"I know about my customers, who they are and who they want to be," he says. "Not everybody went to Harvard or Yale. Not everybody has that perfect pair of old shoes. But," the designer continues, "they're still sophisticated enough to know those things are worth having. A man who becomes an executive wants to look like an executive, no matter where he came from. He wants to look like he's arrived, and look like he's

Lodge. Then it's either breakfast with the family or a ride on Apache, his spotted Appaloosa. Afternoons are spent walking in the hills with Ricky or working with Larry Luke. Dinner is early, and so is bedtime.

Lauren leaves the day-to-day details of running the Double RL to his manager, a former investment adviser who abandoned banking for ranching twelve years ago. Lauren's Colorado neighbors, Luke acknowledges, were initially suspicious and regarded his boss as a city-slick dilettante. But, according to Luke, they don't think that way any longer. "It's the best-run ranch around," he boasts. "Ralph is as professional about this as he is about fashion. We gather our hay before anyone else does, and we have a lot more tonnage. Ralph knows a ranch, like any other business, requires time, investment, and planning. He's giving us all three, and the neighbors can't do anything but respect that."

Moreover, Lauren tries to look the part of a rancher. He loves Western gear and says he feels most comfortable in hand-made boots, worn jeans, and one

been there for a long time.''

Although he's sometimes nervous and has self-doubts, Lauren considers himself one of the first designers to take "original concepts from my own environment" and make them into the kind of clothes these customers wanted.

"I didn't copy Europe," he adds. "I didn't do what Saint Laurent did. I took the pure and the essential, like a blue cashmere sweater with a string of pearls and gray flannel pants, and sent them down a runway. It was a risk. It could have been a total bore. But I believed in it. The simplicity was exciting. And people got it. The fashion press didn't get

it—at least not immediately. And neither did all the stores. But the consumers did.''

Lauren has certainly set trends—the prairie skirt, the Annie Hall and Gatsby looks—but he says he dislikes trendy fashion. "There are designers who look at a sleeve and say, 'Isn't that just the most wonderful sleeve?' I never think about things like that. I want something that doesn't try too hard."

Philosophically, Lauren says he feels closest to Coco Chanel. "It's arrogant to compare myself to Chanel, I know. I don't have her training or her background in the great couture. But there are similarities. I do stand for quality as she did. And style. And I think the women who wear my clothes have great style. They're not fashion people. They're not trendy. They're the same people who like Chanel."

Lauren is also proud of his influence on fashion advertising. "Look at what's going on now," he declares. "It all looks like mine. I started it because I couldn't rely on editorial or store windows to present my world. And my goal was al-

Clockwise from top: The guest house; Dee, queen of the cookhouse, serves breakfast; the cookhouse; Ralph with more of his fleet

ways to present a whole world, not just a pair of pants. Clothes by themselves don't make sense. They need a lifestyle."

That's why he went into home furnishings (selling sheets and pillowcases around themes like "Jamaica" and "Log Cabin") and it's why he decided to build his own shop in New York. This isn't any run-of-the-mill Madison Avenue designer boutique, however. Lauren has taken a twenty-year lease on and restored the Rhinelander Mansion, a landmark building.

The store, opened in 1986, offers Lauren 20,000 square feet of selling space. But he isn't filling it entirely with clothing. The designer wants to sell other things, too, like antiques and his mother-in-law's brownies. And if it will fit, he wants to put an old MG in the window. "I want this to be more than a store—it should be an institution," says Lauren. "I'm not just selling clothes. I'm selling a world, a notion of style. I'm offering a philosophy of life."

—RIDGWAY, COLORADO, 1986

1983

1984   1985

HE TOLD W

Ralph Lauren says he creates for the woman who doesn't want to wear packaged clothes: He simply designs a group of shirts, a group of pants, a group of skirts, and allows his customer to put them together herself.

"My clothes are not uniquely special," he says. "These are normal clothes that are easy to wear, clothes that a woman wants to keep. The woman I design for is not interested in trends."

1979

1986

1984

198

ON CAREER CHIC

"When a woman walks into a room and is not only bright but is dressed appropriately with a dash that makes her look smooth, she has Career Chic," says Ralph Lauren. "She looks beautiful, always special, but not obvious. She has style, but it's not contrived, and she doesn't look like she got up in the morning and worked at it."

Lauren suggests that women who work buy "tailored clothes with an interesting texture, that have a 'forever'-looking quality. They should be clothes that can go out to lunch and then on to a cocktail party when dressed up.

"Stick with subtle clothes so you can change the look," he continues. "Pick muted tones, fabrics that blend, no big plaids . . . and stay away from clothes that make an 'In' or 'Out' fashion statement. My clothes are expensive, but it's investment dressing."

1982

1984

1985

1987

"I am against men's clothes for women—while many of my details are the same, I have the women's clothes made in men's suit factories because they are better equipped to handle the tailoring, but the cut is definitely different. A woman looks sexy if the jacket is cut well."

1982

1985

1985

1985

1982

1980

1980

1981

1979

THE RL ROUTE

Ralph Lauren settles lovingly into the black cockpit of his Porsche Turbo Carrera. Clearly a favorite toy, the car was custom-made to his specifications: Darth Vader black, without a gleam of steel or chrome to break its sleek lines. Lauren loves it. The car definitely has presence. It matches his sunglasses, his bicycle, and the luggage collection he designed to go with it.

In the soft, chill gray of the autumn afternoon, the Porsche lurks like a submarine in the driveway of the beach house. Here Lauren is just plain "Daddy" to his two sons, Andrew and David, and his daughter, Dylan, who, bundled up against the sea breezes, have just finished playing ball with him on the lawn.

But it's Saturday, there are chores to do, and batteries conk out even on the man who made the hacking jacket great. Ralph has to go to a nearby garage to arrange a tow for the dead Land Rover in the driveway.

The Porsche noses slowly out of the compound, but once it hits an open stretch of road, Lauren opens it up. It whines like a 747 on takeoff. "Listen to this sound—it's fabulous," he yells. The whine goes into a roar, and the quiet Long Island countryside goes by in a blur.

"Speed—fast—it's very exhilarating. I don't know if it gets my tension out or what, but it gets my head somewhere else. You really have to be finely tuned, you've got to make all the moments count," he announces, with the kind of gusto usually reserved for beer commercials.

He could easily fit into one of those commercials. In early middle age, Ralph Lauren is in very good shape, physically and financially. Silver-haired and green-eyed, he jogs every morning, and his tight-fitting T-shirt and worn jeans mold the results. Slightly rugged, extremely confident, and moderately macho, he wears a got-it-made aura like a label. But the man behind the label ("I never knew what a designer really was—I thought designers lived on a cloud and sort of draped things around") admits he might easily have chosen a different path.

Raised in the north Bronx, son of a painter of decorative furnishing effects, Lauren grew up in, as he says, "an Ivy League period" that colored his dreams and later influenced his designs.

"I wanted to be a basketball player, but I wasn't tall enough. When I was growing up, I loved movies and I loved a certain style—the kind that goes with a tweedy, rugged, horsey atmosphere. I don't know if the things that inspired me ever existed. I loved Fred Astaire, the Duke of Windsor—they were my inspiration. I wanted to be a teacher at one time. I never thought of money—I thought of loving what I did. I never loved the business world per se. I never loved fashion. I just had style as a kid."

He did, according to Calvin Klein, who grew up in the same area. "I'm younger than Ralph, so we weren't friends, but I remember seeing him around the neighborhood," says Klein. "He always had a sense of style in the way he dressed. He wore army clothes—he would mix them with tweeds and always looked terrific. He had a sense of his own; he stood out more than anyone else."

He still does. As the Porsche slinks through the village on the way home, young girls stop and point. Despite his protestation that "my life is very quiet and very private—I like to be a little out of things," Lauren makes it very hard not to notice him, a characteristic that has marked his career.

Armed with a business degree from New York's City College, Ralph got a job selling men's ties. It was the eve of the wide-tie explosion, and he saw it coming. His company didn't. "I had ideas and they really didn't want to listen to me," he recalls. Another company

did, however, and Lauren began designing ties. Polo was born and Lauren was launched.

"I designed the ties, backed them, and delivered them on Saturdays in a bomber jacket. A lot of stores wanted me to make them narrower, but I wouldn't change because I believed in what I did and stuck with it," he remembers proudly.

There are others who differ with Ralph's assessment of himself, "egomaniac" being one of the most common adjectives that come up. To that Ralph answers, "Anyone who says that really doesn't know me. Believing in yourself and believing that you can do something is not being an egomaniac—it's healthy."

Back in the beach house, Ralph lights a fire and settles down on a couch beside the person who probably knows him best: his wife, Ricky, a warm, vibrant woman with long blondish-brown hair, candid blue eyes, and small, delicate features pointed up by the heavy turtleneck of her navy fisherman's sweater.

A former teacher, she has been married to Ralph since 1964. "Ricky was going to college, teaching at night and working for an eye doctor during the afternoon. I met her at the eye doctor; six months later we were married," recalls Ralph.

Since then, he says, she has been a lot of the inspiration behind his work. "She's the kind of girl who can look good in anything: elegant and chic and rugged and outdoorsy—that's the kind of girl I design for. She's not a fashion girl—she's more active than fashion-conscious. Ricky's not phony in any way. She's involved with me and the kids."

Ricky agrees, insisting that Ralph's "health and his mental stability" are among her greatest concerns. "I wish he'd take it easy, have fun and not take it too seriously, because it is a serious business," she says over a mug of coffee, passing around rich brownies (made by his mother) and fresh apple pie (made by her mother).

Ricky Lauren isn't shy about saying what she thinks. While aware that there are problems that beset many wives of famous men, she claims she hasn't had any. "If I ever feel left out, it's my own problem," she says in a low, forthright voice. "Sometimes I wish I were a little more involved in the technical parts of the business. I am, though, very, very critical of his shows, because he likes it. Somebody has to be honest," she says with a grin.

Ricky also has strong opinions on what she—and other women like her—are doing right now. "From my point of view, a woman having children—that's a career. I'm also working, and this is the work I do.

"It's very nice to be in this position," she continues. "It's like living a fairy tale—at night, dressing up—but it's lovely to know that I can come home to a very solid foundation. I think that's what keeps Ralph sane, too."

Ralph agrees, noting that when the family is at the beach, what they enjoy doing is staying home. "We're taking the option of doing what we really love to do. I love coming home and being home. This is not boring or fake."

He says he really likes relaxing, and most weekends that includes watching movies at home. "I love movies. I've always been inspired by movies, acting, directing—not that I've done it yet, but I'd like to."

Ralph is dead serious. After he was quoted expressing his desire to be an actor ("I know I couldn't become an Al

Ralph and Ricky take a bow

Dinner after the show

IN TOKYO

For Ricky Lauren, the spectacular opener to husband Ralph's Tokyo trip was "a big white bird—an ibis, I think—which flew past our hotel window one morning. Before that, we could have been in Colorado. But that said we were in Japan."

So, too, did the black-tie buffet show sponsored by Lauren's local licensee, Seibu department store. Seibu is spending money, gobs of it, to promote its most important designer name: There are three freestanding Polo shops, the first ever for an American designer in Japan, and a new Seibu store on the Ginza devotes almost an entire floor to Polo products and includes a Coffee Bar with Polo cups.

There is, however, one matter on which they will have to fend for themselves. Although no Bill Blass show in Tokyo is complete without a BB-edition Lincoln Continental lurking in the foyer, Ralph turned down a request from Seibu to bring his pickup truck from Colorado. "I need it at home," explained Ralph.

—TOKYO, 1984

Pacino in three weeks"), agents called to encourage him.

Actually, he already has some of the makings of a natural actor, enhanced by sheer exposure to the show biz aspects of Seventh Avenue and his own role as merchandiser. He instinctively knows, at the click of a camera, how to show himself to advantage.

What roles would he like to play? "I don't think it matters, as long as I get to ride a horse," he jokes, admitting that he wouldn't mind playing a cowboy.

"I was going to say God, in *The Ten Commandments*," teases Ricky.

Why does he think he can do it? "I've never gone to fashion school, but I found my own route," he says simply. "I can do anything I want—and that is a great feeling. I don't think I could ask for anything else."

—EAST HAMPTON, 1978

Ricky and Ralph Lauren
on the veranda

A view of the saltwater pool

The sailcloth-curtained indoor-outdoor dining room

Sun-bronzed, sandal-clad, and grinning beatifically, Ralph Lauren sinks into his sailcloth-cushioned sofa and announces, "This is the closest thing to heaven that I think I can feel."

The sensation Lauren is describing seems to encompass both his contentment with his private Jamaican retreat—an airily elegant house built in the Fifties by financier Clarence Dillon—and his enchantment with the landscape that contains it.

The Laurens' Jamaican hideaway, a tropical fantasy of grainy white walls, rich mahogany moldings, and high tray ceilings, is set some two hundred feet above the sea at a discreet remove from Round Hill's lively resort community.

According to Lauren, the house was "heavy and oppressive" when he discovered it. "We knew it had the bones. It was a wonderful thoroughbred. But it had heavy draperies, black railings, and a musty atmosphere. It was dreary."

With the help of interior designer Angelo Donghia, the Laurens peeled layers of battleship-gray paint from the

THE LAURENS

The living room's stripped-down ... and French doors

Poolside at the Laurens, with a view of the triple-arched porch

The bamboo-furnished living room

moldings and doorframes, deepening their color to mahogany, stripped the drapes from the original regal French doors, added burnished brass fittings, shipped in Deco-ish bamboo furniture and added the requisite sisal and Jamaican-made banana rugs.

The house's languid indoor-outdoor informality is best displayed in its handsome, wide dining-room veranda, which opens onto a sloping expanse of lawn.

New York elements, such as the graceful jardinière that stands near the foyer, are mingled whimsically with the house's own resurrected treasures—most notably a pair of eccentric ceramic tropical birds that flank the fireplace and the smoky gilt-framed mirror that hangs above it. "These are just a little touch of the useless, a bit of the romantic allowance that we give ourselves," says Ricky Lauren, who has just come in from a light rain and is warming herself in one of the crisp, monogrammed linen robes her husband designed expressly to be worn here.

Ricky animatedly guides her visitors to the guest bedroom, a billowy display of hand-painted linen bedclothes and gauze mosquito netting. "This is part of the way Ralph does things," she says. "It's out of the need to realize a dream."

Adds Ralph, "It's private, it's beautiful, and I've earned it."

—MONTEGO BAY, JAMAICA, 1984

IN JAMAICA

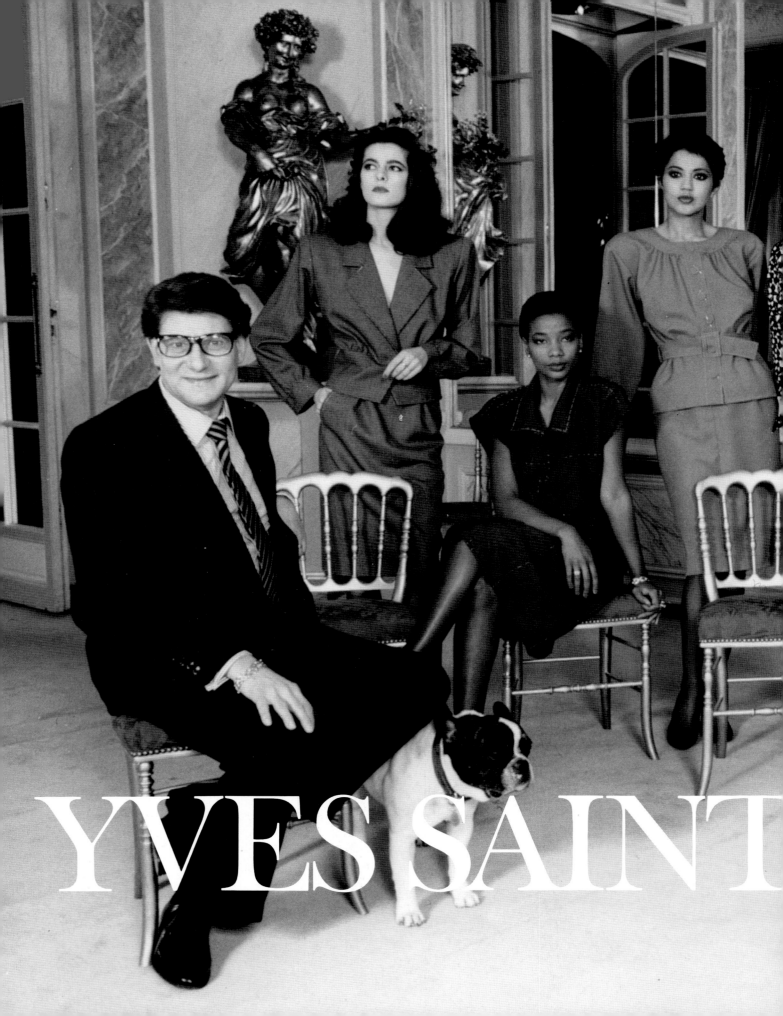

YVES SAINT

It has been said so many times that it scarcely needs repeating, but Yves Saint Laurent remains—unequivocally—the king of fashion, a man who has come to represent modern style and elegance. He walks a delicate tightrope between the everyday and the exotic, and his taste seldom falters; even at his most prosaic, he exudes an effortless sense of polish—reworking the clothes that he himself made classic with new, unexpected counterpoints of color and proportion. It is in the couture—with its endless possibilities for detailed craftsmanship—that he feels most at home, and while he has an uncannily commercial sense for creating clothes that will sell, he leaves the business side of things entirely to his partner, Pierre Bergé.

The alliance is productive. YSL retail sales top $1 billion and the couture house sells an average of 850 to 1,000 pieces each season. There are lavish residences in Normandy, Morocco, Paris, and New York—all furnished, as one might expect, with a sumptuous eye. Saint Laurent has every reason to be complacent. Always, he admits, though, he's propelled by dissatisfaction that gives him his edge over other designers. "Without a doubt, one has to be anguished to be inspired," he says. "The more I work, the more I suffer. And the more I suffer, the greater the success."

LAURENT
The King of Fashion

THE EVOLU TIO

Yves Saint Laurent is celebrating the twentieth anniversary of his couture house. It has been two decades of steadily growing fame, fortune, and influence, but a melancholy YSL says he would prefer to leave the January 1982 date unmarked. "These kinds of things have no interest for me," he insists. "The others get excited, but I can't."

He and business partner Pierre Bergé will throw the appropriate birthday party, at the Lido of all places, and Saint Laurent will, as he puts it, "endure" the festivities, but he would rather be working on his castle in Normandy or reading Proust or editing the thousands of handwritten pages he has penned at night over the past few years. He is not worried that the long-promised book, a mixture of thought and reminiscence, may never be printed.

"I have become a monk," Saint Laurent declares at one point during a wide-ranging interview in his Rue de Babylon apartment. "Going out is my idea of torture. I want to stay at home. When I'm in my bed with a great book, I feel as if nothing else matters." On the few occasions he does venture from his treasure-laden flat, it is to big noisy brasseries, such as La Coupole or Lipp.

After twenty years, he says, his work hasn't gotten any easier; if anything, it is more difficult. "God, when I first started I could work day and night, without stopping for food or rest. It was pure excitement. Now there is this incredible anguish and emptiness before every collection. Something new, something new, always something new. My favorite moment in life has become the moment when the latest collection is finished."

Saint Laurent says his happiest and most productive period was the late Sixties and early Seventies, when he felt in control of his destiny and in step with his generation. Those were the heady days of the Broadway Suit and his Mondrian dresses, his rich-peasant look, those gangster tuxedos, and his tarty Forties collection, which got some fashion editors very upset. The initials YSL were on everyone's lips (and on not so many

products), and he single-handedly made or broke a Paris season.

Saint Laurent began his fashion career in 1954 as an assistant to Christian Dior. When Dior died in 1957, the twenty-one-year-old Saint Laurent, born in Algeria to French parents, was tapped to succeed him. His first collection—the "trapeze" line—was a triumph, and the crowds gathered around the Dior couture house to cheer the shy, skinny boy with the black-rimmed glasses.

But his next few collections, especially his homage to the beat generation, were disappointing, and Dior executives were relieved when YSL was drafted into the French army. After he was discharged, following a nervous breakdown, he met Pierre Bergé, the short, blustery business wizard who had guided

> "For me, the haute couture is a mistress who demands a lot of money. The day she costs me too much, or I fall out of love, I'll envisage other things."

the career of painter Bernard Buffet.

After a series of messy legal suits with Dior, Bergé found a backer, an American named J. Mack Robinson, who put up most of the money for Saint Laurent's first couture house, which was in Passy, a suburb on the outskirts of Paris. The first Yves Saint Laurent collection was presented on February 2, 1962. It, and the three or four that followed, established YSL as the legitimate heir to Balenciaga and Coco Chanel, his favorite designer.

Not every collection has been a great success, but Saint Laurent, as one critic noted, "always goes his own way, usually to be followed a season later by everyone else." When André Courrèges was exciting the fashion press with his miniskirts, Saint Laurent dropped his hems below the knee. When the other big names favored hard-edged Thirties retro looks, YSL turned to romantic Proustian taffetas and Victorian painters' smocks. And when younger design-

OF YSL

At home, 1976

Top: Pierre Bergé and YSL with Wang Hei Di; *far right:* the Chinese Minister of culture; *above right:* outside the exhibit; *above left:* Students "very like" YSL

YSL'S ROAD TO CHINA

EYE "When we saw Pierre Cardin's show here two years ago, we thought that was French design, so simple," said a young official of China's Ministry of Culture. "Now, with Mr. Saint Laurent's, we see that it is not so simple."

Here at the invitation of the Minister of Culture, Saint Laurent ventured forth from his standard double room at Beijing's newest and nicest hotel, the Jianguo, for just one morning's excursion, to the Forbidden City, which once housed China's emperors and their entourages, in the heart of what was once called Peking.

YSL was whisked off in a Red Flag limousine, with Pierre Bergé in a second Red Flag, perched jauntily on the jump seat with one elbow hanging out the window.

A ninety-minute walking tour of the Forbidden City and its palace grounds catapulted YSL into a playful mood. He perched on a bicycle, sat down on a stone floor with a quartet of young Chinese men, and shocked the ever-present American tourists, one of whom stumbled down the four-hundred-dred-year-old steps to the Temple of Harmony declaring, "I've got to find my wife. Oh my God."

Saint Laurent seemed genuinely awed by the palace and grounds, declaring at one point that "no lecture can replace being here to experience this yourself." He was particularly struck by the tableaux, one of which, a simple motif, perfectly matched the tones in his tie.

The same morning took Saint Laurent to other more recent icons to China's past: the Tsien Mien Square portrait of Mao Zedong, and a pedirickshaw. But he beat a hasty retreat to the car when an overbearing traffic cop started berating the assemblage of Chinese who gathered whenever he stopped for photos.

The next day, while young Beijing was crowding into the retrospective exhibition, to which most of them brought sketch pads, Saint Laurent visited the fashion school of the Central Academy of Fine Arts. At the heart of the visit was YSL's hour-long critique of the sketches of a score of promising young art students, who less than a decade ago would have been jailed for such activity. "I don't look at the past," YSL said at one point. "I only look to China's future."   —BEIJING, 1985

ers hit upon shaped and sculptured clothes, YSL went classic and classy.

Robinson eventually sold his interest in YSL to Lanvin–Charles of the Ritz, the American cosmetics conglomerate, but Saint Laurent and Bergé managed to obtain their independence a few years later by surrendering all but nominal rights to perfume and cosmetics. In 1966 they opened the first Rive Gauche boutique, on the Rue de Tournon, since followed by 159 more from Tokyo to Toledo. More than 200 licensees, covering 50 products, now carry the Saint Laurent name.

The two men are very rich indeed.

Saint Laurent says he continues to work for only one reason: the hundreds of people he employs. "I don't care if they take everything away," he declares, waving a hand about the sitting room festooned with paintings by Picasso and Léger. "This kind of life doesn't interest me anymore. I work because I have to— not to make money, but for the people who depend on me. If I don't create the next collection, and the collection after that, they will end up on the streets."

At the end of the interview, dusk has fallen and the room is darkly lit. Bergé's chubby black-and-white French bulldog, Moujik, is snorting fitfully next to YSL, who sips iced mineral water and inhales cigaret after cigaret. The Moroccan servants quietly pad about, filling glasses with a precise, practiced ease. It's an eerie scene, made even eerier by Saint Laurent's sudden pronouncement that he doesn't feel free. "I used to be free, a long time ago," he muses. He wants to explain more, but stops himself. "I guess I'll never be content," he adds, and just smiles. A long, sad smile.

• •

LOOKING BACK: 1974 The couture is in decline—"it won't last another seven years," says Saint Laurent, his brow knit with a sadness and a perverse smile playing on his lips. The lavish new Second Empire house on the Avenue Marceau is Saint Laurent's way of giving the couture a lovely place to die.

But it's also the fortress for the business with which he intends to outlive the couture—in high style. The model for the salon, Saint Laurent explains, "was the salon of Princess Mathilde, the aunt of Napoleon the Third, who had a townhouse on the Rue de Berri."

People who know Saint Laurent only tangentially would think that his

1985

1982

1981

1987

1976

1979

1980

1981

1980

heart would be set on a house in the style of the Twenties, because he was one of the first fashionable persons interested in Art Deco and his apartment is almost an Art Deco museum. But Saint Laurent has always been a sampler of different tastes.

"I'm very eclectic. I change taste rapidly. I think that the couture needs some kind of background such as Napoleon the Third—after all, pure couture is an art of the past. And, after all, that was a very happy period."

Napoleon III also appeals to Yves's love of theatricality. At the recent exhibition of his theater-costume drawings, Saint Laurent said that if he weren't in fashion he would have tried to do something in the theater.

Saint Laurent says he's stuck on, or stuck with, his profession, even though he recognizes that clothes have become far less important than they used to be. He is determined to keep doing couture as long as possible, even if it loses money. "Hopefully, we won't get any new customers. I like to dress the people I like—a clientele of intelligent women.

"Fashion is less intense these days," he says. "It has less importance. And I don't think its importance will come back. What will be more and more important is to be able to create, through a style, clothing that won't go out of style, which can blend in with things of past seasons, give women a wardrobe like a man's wardrobe."

"So long as couture can survive, I'll do all I can to keep it up. What's more important is licensing—but only of things related to my interest in clothes, in fashion, not just a Saint Laurent label on anything. Do I like my profession? It's...well, it's like you don't choose your family."

LOOKING BACK: 1980 Yves Saint Laurent says he is searching for peace—in his life, in his work, in everything. As he sits in his Hotel Pierre suite in New York, looking fit and rested after a month-long vacation in Marrakech, he reflects on his new outlook.

"I needed this vacation," he says, beaming. "I was so tired because I hadn't had a real vacation in so long. I began to work when I was very young, over twenty-two years ago. Sometimes I don't want to continue. But then I realize that this is my life. Now I feel better. I love the gardens, the trees, the earth in Marrakech. I'm beginning to think of things like that now. Before I was too much in the skies. Perhaps it's the age. Now I am attached to nature, the basics."

The change of attitude, he says, is good for him. He claims he has been too retiring, too alone during the past few years. Now he is seeking a "real communication" with people, to move closer to his friends. "Now I need that kind of relationship," he says, again adding, "It's the age."

Not that Saint Laurent considers himself old. "I am young in spirit. But I was too young, even three years ago. Now I have a man's maturity. I am not a young lion now. I'm an old lion." And then he adds with that broad, sly, typically YSL grin, "Perhaps a fox.

"I have learned to respond to the basic things in my life," the designer continues. "To find oneself is the best thing you can offer to others. I give more and more now, not only in fashion but in life.

"I have become a very serious man. And for me, it's a great joy."
—PARIS, 1982, 1974, 1980

1982

1979

1987

"Sometimes I am disgusted by the copies. Everybody copies me. I am not being pretentious, but it is like they are taking something profound in me, like a thief. They capture the sense of Saint Laurent, but they don't capture me.

"And then sometimes I don't care. I like people more and more now. I'm not preoccupied with other designers and their work. I'm just an old fox who knows a lot of things they don't."

1981

1981

1974

1980

The Opium Wars

With less than two weeks to go and thousands of details still to work out, things began falling apart. The problem was a lot more delicate than hoisting a thousand-pound buddha onto the deck of a rented ship, or where the decorator could buy five thousand white cattleya orchids and stay within budget.

No, the problem that Friday, when everybody's message pad looked like a chain letter, seemed almost insurmountable. Over five hundred invitations had been hand-delivered, six television stations were sending reporters, and Marina Schiano, YSL's lady in New York, was mad.

The reason for her displeasure was not readily apparent, although the thrust of her temper was. If she did not get her way, and by that she meant if the wishes of the House of Saint Laurent were not honored, well then, YSL just wouldn't come. It was that simple.

It was also the ultimate weapon, all but silencing the already shell-shocked executives of Charles of the Ritz. It was bad enough that Marina had shrieked and bullied them into submission; that Saint Laurent had chosen Opium as the name for his newest perfume; that they were a division of a staid old drug company called Squibb. All that, even the cost of the launch party, could be coped with, survived. But if Saint Laurent and his entourage didn't show, if Charles of the Ritz, God forbid, was stuck hosting this waterside extravaganza...

What would the buyers say?

Days later, a truce had been reached. The gospel, according to Dick Furlaud, Squibb chairman and YSL admirer, was this: Let Marina have her way. This is YSL's party. Charles of the Ritz should just shut up and pay.

Which did not mean that the fighting would not continue, or the mechanics of giving a black-tie cocktail party for eight hundred (on a boat, in a seedy part of downtown Manhattan) would be smooth. After all, there were special considerations in giving this kind of a party; most important, on every point YSL had to approve.

So from the very beginning there were problems, from the day Cathy Cash Spellman, of the Spellman Advertising Agency, suggested that Ritz rent an old boat, the *Peking*. As time wore

On board the *Peking*

YSL with Pauline Tregère and Bergé....

Marina Schiano....

DV et al.

on, giving a party by committee would prove tedious and then exhausting. In the chain of command: YSL, Pierre Bergé, Schiano, Spellman, and the Charles of the Ritz hierarchy.

When Renny Reynolds, decorator and florist extraordinaire, entered the picture, another transcontinental relationship began. A perfectionist like

YSL, he too had ideas.

Some of Reynolds's rejected proposals: wild animals—lions, panthers, parrots, monkeys, toucans, and cockatoos; gold lamé sails; a real sod lawn planted underneath the highway; a new dance floor for the "disco" deck.

Were Reynolds's ideas too extravagant? Too decadent? Not YSL's taste?

"No," said Marina confidentially. "Renny is a nice, nice boy and very professional. But he had to understand our image, the dignity of Saint Laurent."

The Image is a matter of Marina's subjective interpretation, almost impossible to second-guess. The distribution of thousands of "hip" fortune cookies was rejected as "tacky," but a $30,000 Zambelli fireworks display (that's 7,000 Chinese, French, and Italian fireworks shot from two barges in the East River and electronically programmed to twenty minutes of music, with the YSL logo as the grand finale) was not.

The Image also demanded:
• Eight hundred invitations printed by the Mafia Press in Paris and flown here for calligrapher Nancy Westheimer to address ($2.50 an envelope) and the Mobil Messenger Co. to hand-deliver ($1,500).
• A generous donation to the South Street Seaport Museum so that its 350-foot boat, the *Peking,* could be painted,

repaired, and made exclusive to YSL for two months prior to the party.
• Six models to follow YSL around and wear his Opium Fantasy clothes.

The Image also is tied up with the Attitude, and Schiano defines it thus: "If you wouldn't serve Almaden in your home, you wouldn't serve it at your party."

Now, no one knows if it's the Image or the Attitude that's causing the Trouble, but both seem to stick in the craw of Charles of the Ritz. The invitation to Estée Lauder is a perfect example. As a loyal couture customer, Lauder could not possibly be omitted. But as a Charles of the Ritz competitor, even Estée could understand the problem.

Fortunately, the food and liquor proved to be less of a dilemma. With the exception of a few personal requests from YSL (he loves Bollinger Champagne and cucumber sandwiches), the menu from Glorious Food was "heavy" cocktail fare and included 13,000 oys-

ters, clams, and marinated mussels (served in a six-foot-high ice sculpture of a clam); 160 pounds of veal and steak, for veal and steak tartare; 50 pints of strawberries, and 2,500 miniature fruit tartlets.

The liquor was based on the consumption of 7,200 glasses. For the thirsty: 30 cases of Bollinger Champagne; 30 cases of Pinot Chardonnay; five cases of Johnny Walker Red; three cases of Beefeater Gin; two cases of Jack Daniel's; two cases of Canadian Club; one case of dry vermouth; 6 bottles of Dubonnet; and 6 bottles of sherry.

Of course, Reynolds, who was in charge of music, lighting, flowers, and decorations, had the weightiest problem of all. The ambience he creates—with YSL's sketches, don't forget—can make or break a party.

Aware of this, Renny flexed the Far East of the Imagination. He conceived such spectacular sights as hundreds of hand-lacquered parasols, fans, and live bamboo trees; an eighteen-foot-high YSL arch at the entrance to the boat's gangplank; an Oriental garden with thousands of white cattleya orchids; a five-foot-high, thousand-pound buddha mounted on a five-foot platform; a fifty-by-fifty-foot grosgrain rug designed by YSL; fifty YSL banners, twenty feet high and five feet wide, flapping from the boat's yardarms; thousands of hand-made goose-down pillows on which guests could sit and watch a troupe of Chinese acrobats.

The details that remained—the rain tents (which took two weeks to rig), the insurance (enormous), the fireworks permits (from four city agencies plus the Coast Guard), the gifts (Opium perfume plus YSL's Opium poem in a limited edition), the security (six private guards to begin watch forty-eight hours prior to the party), and the traffic control—had been running everyone ragged.

But if the effort seemed mind-boggling, can you imagine the price? Such aggravation is not purchased cheaply.

The "official" price (and that was extracted in delicate surgery) is $100,000, although well-placed sources put it closer to $250,000.

For a more accurate appraisal, a call was placed to Squibb chairman Furlaud. He thought both figures "grossly exaggerated," but said, "Of course, I don't know. As far as I'm concerned, this is purely a social occasion."

—NEW YORK, 1978

A vegetable still life and other party fare

The thousand-pound Buddha

The entrance to Dar Es Saada

The garden with its circular fountain

Relaxing with Hazel

FANTASY LIVING

Like many of the treasures of Morocco, Dar Es Saada is a hidden one. You can approach it from any angle and not see the rich pink building behind the high, thick walls that surround it. There is a Texaco gas station next door. Scruffy children play with stray cats on the street outside. A small Moroccan walks past, carrying a live sheep on his back. A camel undulates its way across the road.

Once admitted past the formidable pink walls through a somewhat forbidding cedar door, it's a different story. You are faced with a large circular courtyard and a softly angular structure sprawling splendidly in the middle of a state-park-sized garden. Five low, wide steps lead to a massive bronze door that is framed by two large Art Decoratif–Moroccan pillars. The door opens to a seemingly endless foyer and a smiling houseboy in an impeccable white cotton costume.

Once you are over the initial impact of the structural beauty of the place, the mood of Saint Laurent's Marrakech sinks in. His taste and touch are everywhere. Dar Es Saada, which took three years to renovate and decorate, incorporates his love of Moroccan Islamic splendor with his regard for clean, graphic good taste.

Within the house there is an overriding sense of grandeur, but you don't feel a stuffy "look but don't touch" atmosphere because of YSL's casual touches. Upstairs in the garden room, for example, he has juxtaposed comparatively inexpensive rattan furniture with priceless antique Moroccan artifacts. In another room he accessorized chaises with amusing feather and leather African fans, and baskets serve as minibars.

"It's a home built for its setting," says Saint Laurent. "It fits with a nostalgic, romantic country." It is also a home fit for comfort. It includes nine separate living environments, multiple terraces, a pool, a large pond, a fountain, and an oasis of a garden.

Saint Laurent and Bergé employ two gardeners, one guard, one cook, two chambermaids, two manservants, and various other help when needed. A carriage driver will be added when they buy a horse and carriage, the acceptable means of transportation for wealthier Marrakech residents ("Not at all a tourist thing," Bergé cautions).

The home is thoroughly but not totally Moroccan. Saint Laurent, Bergé, and interior designer Bill Willis have added touches of Persia, Syria, nineteenth-century England, and the French Art Deco period.

Color is probably the first thing you notice about the structure, which is built of tetlah, a native material that, when highly polished, gives the appearance of pale, delicate marble. The stone floors are flesh-colored: "Just like a woman's skin," Saint Laurent says.

Life at Dar Es Saada is usually languid and rarely lazy. Bergé and Saint Laurent are habitually up at 8 A.M. After coffee, Saint Laurent works on his book-in-progress and Bergé reads, swims, or attends to the constantly ringing telephone.

At 10:30 this day, YSL appears on the terrace in a white cotton caftan. He wears nothing underneath. He accepts a compliment on his haircut. "I cut it myself." He laughs. "I needed a cut and didn't have a barber here, so I just took the scissors and did it."

Before lunch, there is usually a swim in the tiled pool. If it is August, one doesn't spend too much time sunbathing—"unbearable," says Saint Laurent. It's safer to don one of the flat-crowned, brimmed straw hats Saint Laurent bought in the souks. He says the hats remind him of Chanel.

Lunch and dinner are usually served in the dining room—a rustic oblong room with a long parqueted table designed by Bill Willis, and a graphic side table designed by YSL. The table setting is plain: solid Moroccan pottery plates, unembellished silverware, pale lavender napkins, and Saint Laurent's hand-painted snake-motif glasses. The cuisine is almost always Moroccan. A favorite meal starts with a vegetable, coriander, and hot pepper mixture, followed by chicken with lemon and olives, a classic Moroccan dish, then a selection of cheeses and mosque-shaped ice cream.

For after-lunch coffee, YSL leads the way to the garden, where the manservants have spread out an immense soft red tapestry on the grass. Moroccan trays are filled with coffee urns, cups, saucers, and several packages of Kool cigarets.

Bergé sits upright, taking pictures with his Olympus OM2 camera, and Yves settles down on several of the eighteenth-century Turkish-tapestry-cov-

ered pillows. The only noises come from the dragonflies, birds, and bees in the garden. Hazel, YSL's constant companion of a dog, yawns. "Poor Hazel," says Saint Laurent suddenly. "She was kidnapped recently. She was out walking in the street and some men grabbed her up and put her in a sack. It was unbelievable that we found her twenty-four hours later—with the same men—in a plastic bag. Imagine spending twenty-four hours in a plastic bag. She was completely traumatized." The Chihuahua stretches.

After coffee, YSL stops to point out one of his favorite rooms, the place that most effectively reflects his love of *art*

Here and left: the lily pond

decoratif. "It has a timeless, seasonless quality," he muses quietly. Yves explains that there are no flowers in the room, nor in any other room of the house. "I don't think this place has need of flowers," he says. "The only time there are flowers in the house is during winter when the Moroccan roses bloom. The size is unbelievable. And they don't exist anywhere but in Morocco."

On afternoons when he is not writing, Saint Laurent may take a trip to the Place Djemara El Fna and the souks. There you feel the undercurrents of the city, which dates back to 1062, when it was founded by a Saharan nomad. The souks assault one's senses with the scents of kif, new leather, and natural henna, the taste of sticky tea à la menthe, the look of brilliantly dyed yarns and sunscorched pink buildings, and the hawking of hundreds of merchants. Bergé and Saint Laurent have a greater enthusiasm for the souks than do most tourists.

On winter evenings, the fireplaces are lit. In Marrakech, December nights are as cold as the days are hot. "It's wonderful here in the winter," says Saint Laurent. "You spend the day in the hot sun and the cold nights by the fireplace." —MARRAKECH, 1976

YSL dressed à la Marrakech

A Syrian mother-of-pearl chest

A guest room with a tiled fireplace and a Morocco-woven rug

The garden room with carved Morrocan pieces and cedar and glass doors

★★★★ Nancy Kissinger, a long drink of water, in YSL

★★★★ LouLou Klossowski, hot haute

★★★ Estée Lauder, Mother Beauty, in YSL

★★★ The transformed pool room at the Met

★★ Jackie de Ribes, always faithful, in YSL

★★★ Pat Buckley, Mrs. America, in Blass

★★★ Marie-Hélène de Rothschild in YSL—coup de foudre, with ★★ Olympia de Rothschild in YSL—lacey

★★ Paloma Picasso in YSL with FV hair

Louise Goes to the Great Yves-ning at the Met

I've always loved being conquered by Frenchmen, ever since I met my first Rothschild in the Thirties. So naturally I couldn't wait to be ravished again by the all-time seducer of fashion, Yves Saint Laurent, at the Metropolitan Museum gala in his honor. And indeed, though Yves is as timid as they come in some ways, that evening he quietly but forcefully (be still my heart) took New York with the Gallic authority of a Napoleon, at a four-star event that brought class back to the Met.

The dinner and dance was the sort of party that had Bill Blass commenting that it genuinely had the feeling of a private dinner, in spite of the guest list of 810 for dinner, with 2,500 arriving later for gawking and dancing. With each dinner ticket at $500 (and $100 for the late set), it was a financial as well as a social success, netting the Met a cool half million.

And if someone had thought to take up a jewelry collection at just one of the better dinner tables, they could have upped that figure by at least $3 million. While I, of course, always fondly think of the evening as the night every major jewel came out of the vaults, it was much the Night of the Frogs. As the Met's Sisi Cahan put it, "It's as if they turned Paris on its side, and the whole city slid over."

YSL friends, fans, and followers left *gai Paris* in droves, though I saw neither envious hide nor hair of Hubie, Karl, Emanuel, Marc, or Alix. Shame, French designers! Where is your spirit of camaraderie? After all, generous-spirited Bill Blass and Oscar de la Renta broke bread at Yves's own table. And Valentino, Hanae Mori, and Zandra Rhodes journeyed from distant lands to hail the King of Fashion. Calvin Klein, on the other hand, didn't even make the trip through Central Park—perhaps he was delayed there by a mugger or a jogger.

Among those who did show, however, a festive harmony prevailed, though there are always a few trouble-makers at an event so fraught with social politics. It took some juggling for Susan Gutfreund—who's barreling up the ladder, as they say—to be satisfied with her placement. And—ah, sweet romance—devoted Babs Davis couldn't bear to be apart from her husband, Big Fox Marvin. In order for the Love Foxes to sit together, Noble Nancy Kissinger had to move to another table.

I myself was secretly pining to sit at the premier table of Yves, where everything—I gather—was très drôle. The seating there was royal flush: King Yves, flanked by Vicomtess Jackie de Ribes and Baroness Marie-Hélène de Rothschild (who, I hear, was doing very witty imitations of her table mates). Then there were Baron Guy de Rothschild; Empress "Ruby" Vreeland (ruby cheeks, ruby mouth, and ruby-studded YSL evening sweater); Evangeline

Bruce, the Queen of Washington; Annette Reed, the Queen of Fun; Bill Paley, the King of Communications; LouLou Klossowski, the Queen of the Atelier; Gustav Zumsteg, the King of Silk; and Blass and de la Renta, American Lords of the RBs.

The highlights in Yves's corner: the dramatic fight for chocolate between the Queen of Washington and the Queen of Fun and Bill Paley's obvious infatuation with four-star LouLou.

K of C Bill, who arrived with the Q of W, got to exchange a sizzling embrace with the Queen of "Dallas," Linda Gray, who plays the slut Sue Ellen. When de la Renta had asked Gray if she wanted to meet Bill, Linda purred, "Of course. He pays my rent." "Finally, we meet," she said, as she slithered over to K of C Bill in skintight Bob Mackie sequins. I awarded her performance four Nielsen stars, a rating I'm sure Bill would share.

Yves was so awed by the whole event that when he met lovely Linda and chin-up Carol Burnett, he confused one with the other and told Carol how much he loved her in "Dallas." Vreeland, in the meantime, was booming, "It's got guts, doncha think?" of the exhibit.

And sentimental Gustav Zumsteg—who I understand becomes misty-eyed at the drop of a bolt of fabric—was saying, "It's moving for me, because it's not only a retrospective of Yves's fashion, but of my fabrics." He added, looking at the 15,000 yards of the fabric he'd donated—artfully draped to transform the Pool Room—"What a shame it all has to come down in three hours."

The room was sumptuous—all in Yves's favorite color combinations of fuchsia, red, and orange. "The rose, the rose," swooned La Belle Hélène Rochas. Four-star Nancy Kissinger fantasized, "I wish I could do an apartment that quickly." And chairwoman Pat Buckley, who'd been up till 4:30 that morning tying on golden bows and pleating curtains, said, in response to a compliment, "It may be a success, but I need seventy-five face lifts and monkey glands."

The dinner itself—gloriously executed by Glorious Foods (really, dinner for 810 is no easy trick)—started with coquilles Saint Jacques, then veal-wrapped cold fillet of beef, French bread with cheese, and chocolate cake. The wines were Macon Lugny les Charmes, Château Greysac Médoc, and, for Champagne, Cordon Rouge Brut. There were 50 cases of each, all donated by Mumm's. The tab for the dinner came to around $80,000. I understand a large part of the evening's tab was underwritten by Charles of the Ritz, which, as everyone knows, does YSL's fragrances.

There was all sorts of dishy speculation, from the méchantes tongues, about who looked better, the French or the American women. I myself am a fashion democrat and divided my scant four-star ratings among a Frenchwoman, chère LouLou; an American, dear Nancy K; and Diana Vreeland (God knows where she comes from!).

And while for most of the homage-paying ladies it was strictly dresses by Yves, Pat Buckley (Mrs. America) explained her choice of Blass: "I'm the American chairwoman at an event at an American museum—the greatest museum in the world; therefore I chose to wear an American dress. I'm sure Yves understands."

—LOUISE J. ESTERHAZY,
New York, 1982

YSL: Introspective

I'm afraid to even think about it," Yves Saint Laurent says. "All those people, all those parties, all those journalists. And then, of course, there's the biggest worry of all: What will I do afterward?"

Surrounded by vases of orchids and lilies, and several million dollars' worth of paintings, Saint Laurent sits in the salon of his Paris apartment reflecting on what it's like to be the first living designer honored with a retrospective exhibition at the Metropolitan Museum of Art in New York. "I'm not going there as a triumphant conqueror," he jokes. "I'm very modest."

In fact, Saint Laurent seems a bit dazed by it all. "Of course I'm flattered," he suggests. "But I have a feeling that this represents an enormous watershed in my career. I don't know what might hit me on the head when it's over. But I'll probably end up going back to my little atelier with Mounia [his favorite model] and a few pieces of mousseline and starting the next collection."

A week before the opening-night gala, Saint Laurent arrived in New York and saw the exhibition for the first time. Although he had helped Diana Vreeland, special consultant to the Costume Institute at the Met, choose the dresses, he had kept himself removed from the "little details."

"I didn't have to spend much time with Diana because I have the utmost confidence in her," he explains. "At first, she can be worrying, of course. She comes in looking weary and tired and waits for an hour and then you wonder, 'What's happening?' Then, suddenly, she jumps up, runs around, and chooses exactly the right dresses. No disagreements. Everything is picked perfectly."

YSL is particularly pleased that Vreeland decided to include a group of dresses from the Rive Gauche ready-to-wear in the show. "Anyone can wear them. Women on the street. People from Florida," he says. "That's intelligent. It makes the exhibition much more modern."

1979

1983

The exhibition, YSL says, has taught him a few things about himself. After seeing Duane Michals's photographs of the chosen clothes, he was astonished to find that, "with one or two exceptions," all the dresses could still be worn today. "People have always said you can wear a YSL dress season after season, but I never saw it. They really do have a timeless feeling."

On reflection, he says he prefers his latest collections to his earliest. "The more recent ones are more striking," suggests YSL, "because they have more technique and maturity. There's an evolution in my cuts that you can see in the shoulders and the suits."

His favorite collections: "The first one I did for Dior and the last one I did for Dior," he says with a wry smile, referring to the avant-garde collection that led to his break with the house. "That was when I introduced knits and leather to the couture." Other favorites: "the Broadway Suit collection and the Picasso."

Over the years YSL has been inspired by countless heroines. He mentions Marlene Dietrich ("because of the way she wore pants"), Pauline de Rothschild, Bette Davis, Joan Crawford, Catherine Deneuve, and Marilyn Monroe. He also draws ideas from fictional characters such as Emma Bovary, the Duchess de Guermantes, Odette Swann, and Desdemona from *Othello*.

But YSL says it is his mannequins that have always brought his ideas to life. "They are the bulls and I am the toreador. Their bodies either live or die when they wear a dress for the first time," observes YSL.

His other inspiration, the street, holds less allure these days. "Clothes depend on events. But today the street seems all an exaggeration of what we've seen since the era of the black blouson," he says, summing up the image of the Sixties. "Today the street is negative, dirty, and dumb, and above all senseless. I don't go out much, but if I see one or two punks, that's enough to understand."

YSL came to New York with sever-

> "When Yves was young, he was a prince. Now he's king of the fashion world since Chanel died. Even if somebody else tries to catch the crown, Yves is still there."—Pierre Bergé, business partner of Yves Saint Laurent

1980

1982

al members of what he calls "my family," chief among them Pierre Bergé. LouLou Klossowski, whom Saint Laurent describes as "charm, poetry, excess, extravagance, and elegance all in one blow," also traveled with him, as did Anne Marie Munoz ("my favorite hand"), several other of his atelier assistants, and Gustav Zumsteg of Abraham, the fabric manufacturer.

YSL's personal decorator, Jacques Grange, had come to New York earlier to organize the décor for the opening-night festivities and to spruce up Saint Laurent and Bergé's New York apartment, making it, he says, "warmer, like an Englishman's club or the home of a man who's returned from adventures in India and Africa."

Jacqueline de Ribes, now a YSL competitor, also flew in from Paris and hosted a dinner for about fifty at Mortimer's, which followed a reception the French Consulate had to show off two hundred of YSL's theatrical costumes and scenery designs.

Despite rumors to the contrary, YSL is not yet ready to publish his long-awaited autobiography. "I haven't done anything about it for a while," sighs Saint Laurent. During his Morocco holidays, however, he did write his first short story. "It's about a man who meets a woman in a bar," he explains cryptically. He also spent much of his vacation hunting for antique daggers, his latest fa-

vorite hobby. He already has knives with bejeweled and crystal handles, and this time he discovered one carved in jade. "I don't know why I love these things," he wonders, brandishing his sharp acquisition like a boy playing pirate.

When asked, however, what gift he would most like to receive, YSL turns solemn. "A cross," he answers instantly. Why? "Because I'm a believer. And it helps me a lot in difficult times to be a believer. If someone gave me a cross, I could wear it, and it would be more precious than any other object I have lying around," he says, gesturing dismissively toward the Légers, the Picassos, and even the Goya.

—PARIS and NEW YORK, 1983

1980

1985

1986

"Basics are the real modern touch of my métier, my success. Even though I do things with more fantasy, I'm more interested in a blazer, to continue it each year with a new cut, a new perfection."

1983

1985

First Dior collection

1976

1984

1986

1986

1986

1980

1984

1983

1985

1982

1986

1985

1985

1985

The stone entry gate

YSL at the entrance to the 100-year-old chateau

REMEMBRANCE OF THINGS PAST

"It's my folly," sighs Yves Saint Laurent on a Sunday tour of his neo-Gothic retreat in Normandy. "This place is one of the craziest ideas I've ever had."

The house, grandly christened the Château Gabriel when it was built 110 years ago, was purchased three years ago and is still far from completed. There is more furniture to buy for a few of its twenty or so rooms, a rose garden to plant, and twelve fireplaces to unclog. A half dozen workmen and a team of gardeners are laboring to put the sixty-acre estate in order.

Nonetheless, Saint Laurent has decided he likes the house, finished or not. "It's quiet and comforting," says the designer, who is making his first winter visit here. "One's never sure about a house until you see it in a bad season."

Pierre Bergé, on the other hand, had no doubts. His first command was to install a red-brick helicopter pad on the grounds so he could pilot his spanking-new, all-white AS 355 helicopter from Paris, a twenty-five-minute flight. Once the pad was completed, Bergé began to make the 130-mile journey for brief inspections and to check on his stable of prizewinning horses and herd of brown-and-white cattle. The latter, he admits, serve no other function than to "look great with the house."

It's the kind of unlikely detail that makes perfect sense at Château Gabriel, where no expense has been spared to create a mind-boggling Proustian fantasy. Every stick of furniture is mint-condition nineteenth-century, many of the wall coverings and furnishing fabrics were specially made in Lyons from Victorian patterns, and almost every visible sign of the 1980s has been ruthlessly banished (except in the kitchen).

Moreover, the bedrooms bear the names of the main characters from Proust's masterpiece, *Remembrance of Things Past*, starting with YSL's three-room suite called Swann. "He was the hero, of course," quips Saint Laurent.

"It was Yves's idea to name the rooms and to try to make them bear more than a passing resemblance to the characters," explains Jacques Grange, the interior designer charged with carrying out the work. "We bought most of the furniture in France, but it has taken more than two years to find. With Yves and Pierre, you know, everything has to be just right."

The ground floor, which includes the dining room, two salons, and an extraordinary winter garden, was the first completed. The salons are dominated by the floor-to-ceiling oak and graystone fireplaces that were built with the house. Their furnishings—a Directoire desk and loden-green velvet card table, deep burgundy and bright red velvet couches and low chairs, yellow-striped taffeta shades—are plush and surprisingly comfortable.

The rooms, insist Grange, "aren't meant to be a museum," but they do manage to suggest, in their exquisite detail, why it was that the nineteenth-century country gentry liked to pass so many evenings at home.

The dining room, as sumptuous as any of the others, runs the length of the house and contains two tables: One, which can accommodate up to twenty, is meant for large-scale entertaining, while a smaller round table in an alcove at the end of the black-and-white-tiled room is reserved for lunches and more intimate occasions. The tables are served by dumbwaiter from the basement kitchen, presided over by Christian, Bergé, and Saint Laurent's chef since the early Seventies.

Before meals, drinks are usually served in the winter garden, Saint Laurent's favorite room. Grange copied the ceiling from one in the Brighton Pavilion, Edward VII's old hangout, and the long, glass-encased garden is packed with more than thirty varieties of plants and ferns, which Jean, the head gardener, replaces with new recruits from the hothouse every few weeks. "Plants need vacations just like everybody else," says the passionate Jean.

But it isn't really the plants or the room's pleasant furniture that gives the winter garden its unique charm. It's the magnificent view, which Saint Laurent describes as "mesmerizing" and Bergé claims was "the main reason we bought the house. You're inside but feeling outside," says Saint Laurent. "The light differs from second to second, and I can change the plants to fit my mood. I sometimes sit here for hours just gazing into the winter mist."

The garden faces a long, open terrace, and when weather permits the huge double doors are left open for guests to wander in and out. The large brick terrace, in turn, overlooks Château Gabriel's park, which contains its own lake as well as those highly decorative cows grazing in the distance. Beyond the park's rolling hills is Deauville, three miles away, and beyond the town is an unhindered view of the open sea.

On good days, which are notoriously few in wintertime Normandy, Bergé and Saint Laurent can see the outline of Le Havre, fifty miles to the north. "When you can't see Le Havre, you know it's raining."

All three bedrooms on the second floor share the spectacular panorama. The most feminine in the house has been named Guermantes, after Proust's impeccably elegant and aristocratic duchess. "I had LouLou [Klossowski] in mind when I was looking for the furniture," explains Grange as he smooths the pure silk coverings on the canopied bed. Grange had a Lyons atelier working full time for six months on the fringed curtains for this bedroom and the eight others in the house.

Next door is Bergé's sumptuous lair, code-named Charlus by YSL. Charlus was a blustery baron, infatuated with his own virility, and his personality shows through in the spacious bedroom with its unfussy colors, comfortable leather chairs, and ten-foot-long bookcase. The room, which Grange considers the "most astonishing" in the house, is festooned with Bergé's collection of "noble Moor" paintings. The huge Charlus bathroom with walls partially covered in trompe l'oeil mahogany is equally impressive.

A bedroom, a study, and a narrow connecting library, as well as a rather sedately sized bathroom, at least compared to the other eight in the house, make up Saint Laurent's suite. "It's a refuge," says YSL, who likes to spend afternoons composing poetry and collecting thoughts on a portable typewriter

Chateau Gabriel

atop his imposing Directoire desk.

YSL's bedroom is done in rich, dark shades, and has a smallish nineteenth-century bed over which hangs a wooden cross. Grange used the same dark fabric for the walls of the study, which has bigger windows and more light, though both rooms are filled with silver candelabra. In one corner Saint Laurent has placed an enormous nineteenth-century artist's portfolio in leather, and in another a perfect gold swan. The only painting is by Nernet Lecomte, a portrait done in 1860 of a French princess in Arab costume. "The perfect Saint Laurent woman," notes Grange.

The guest rooms on the third floor run the gamut from the pristine simplic-

ity of "Albertine" to the decadent clash of color and print in "Vendurin."

The extensive servants' quarters are in the basement, and near the stables. Bergé is quite proud of this area, and during a recent tour of the château he insisted on showing off the laundry room. "Better than any expensive hotel," he boasted.

There is a separate cottage for the caretaker, who, in addition to his regular duties, looks after Douce the deer and Pauline the goat. There is also a groom to exercise the three racehorses, whose stable is covered with medals and ribbons.

Also in the basement, with its own small entrance, is a room that Saint Laurent and Bergé have had constructed—a classic nineteenth-century room for billiards, a game that, like Swann and Charlus, they are learning to play.

"The only problem," complains Bergé, "is that Yves keeps waiting to hit the red ball. He's just too esthetic."
—Benerville-Sur-Mer, FRANCE, 1983

The Winter Garden

Bergé pays a call

Christian, YSL's chef

Bergé's bath

The desk in Saint Laurent's bedroom

The billiard room

The Madeleine

Giorgio Armani's favorite adjective is "modern." The reigning monarch of Milanese fashion claims, with good reason, that he has taught a woman to dress with the slouchy ease of a man. He works from a repertoire of men's-wear-inspired classics, but he is quick to point out that he always tempers masculine cuts with a feminine edge, whether in the way a jacket moves in at the waist or a lapel drapes invitingly low. His products reap retail sales of well over $100 million a year, a success built with Sergio Galeotti, Armani's longtime business partner, who died in 1985.

An exacting, hard-driven purist, Armani has built himself an ivory-tower existence in Milan, where adjoining palazzos, covered in cool gradations of beige, serve as both workplace and personal place. While he admits to being so cut off that he is not always aware of what's going on in the outside world, the sheer force of his personal vision continues to keep him at the top of the totem pole. In everything from the design of his Mediterranean getaway and Tuscany farmhouse to the cut of a mannequin's hair, he insists on having absolute control. He is, for instance, the only Milanese designer to show impeccably staged collections in his own theater. And backstage before the lights go up, Giorgio can inevitably be found applying the final touches to mannequins' hair.

GIORGIO ARMANI
Modern Italian Chic

t was rumored in Milan that tickets to Giorgio Armani's spring fashion show were being scalped by hotel concierges for $500 and more. Was it true? No one knew for certain, but no one really doubted it either. For there is no show in Milan that is watched like Armani's, that is awaited like Armani's, that wraps its audience in a feeling of spectacle and history-in-the-making like Armani's. He is the King of Milan, the master tailor, the prince in the austere palazzo.

It was just ten years earlier, in October 1975, that Armani had presented his first collection of women's wear: a decade of Armani and already it's inconceivable to imagine what women today would have looked like without his revolutionary influence.

"I realized that the idea of chic is changing, that it has nothing to do with a woman wearing a crêpe de Chine blouse with a bow at the neck," Armani had said a few years after his foray into women's fashion. "Modern chic has nothing to do with old chic."

Modern chic has everything to do with the precise, neat, and sometimes humorous clothes the designer has mastered, repeatedly igniting the fashion press—and customers. Last year retail sales of Giorgio Armani products worldwide brought in $120 million. That includes products from the fourteen companies licensed to make Armani merchandise plus the Armani stores—fourteen Giorgio Armani boutiques and eighty-five Emporio Armani stores.

If one is technical, Armani's creative binge started with his winter 1979 collection, in which he draped a tailored jacket, followed the next season by his one-lapel and strapless blazers.

But, realistically, Armani's creative yearnings started much earlier. Born in 1933 in Pacenza, forty miles southeast of Milan, the second of three children of a transport company manager, Armani entered university with dreams of a medical degree.

"I would have been a terrific doctor," he says. "I have a strong sense of the humane. I wouldn't have gone into a big hospital; I would have done something in a small situation, something personal. But I was completely unable to study. It's not a question of intelligence. It's concentration. All of a sudden I realized I couldn't do it." After three years, his studies ended when he was drafted into the military and served a brief hitch

1981

"I've always made fashion that takes reality into account, as well as the dream to always be better, to look better, to feel better. But it doesn't scorn or disapprove of the world as it is, or women as they really live. You can't make fashion without taking into account the enormous differences that exist between women. Some women are very poor in material goods but can be rich in their lives, in the things that count. And a lot of very rich women lead very poor lives."

1984

1987

1982

1984

1978

1981

1985

1982

1984

as an army medic.

"In the military service I was really nice to everyone," says Armani. "I'd be in a giant mess hall, with everyone shouting, and I'd say, 'Might I have that?' I was so polite everyone noticed. It was my method of getting respect.

"I don't know exactly why that was," he muses. "I never thought of being ambitious, of being rich and famous. I came from a simple family that when they died didn't get written up in the papers. But there was something in me. My esthetic sense was always rebelling. From the time I was a kid I was always thinking of arriving—distinguishing myself from others."

"My tastes are simple in life. I was born into a simple family, and I have worked very hard to have nice things. My success hasn't changed me. You don't see things like seventeenth- or eighteenth-century antiques or art in my house, because it's not me. As I wasn't born an aristocrat, it's useless to try to become one through fashion. I don't want to be too distant from my roots. It's only important to be modern in my work, and honest."

In 1954 Armani, out of the service, took a job with La Rinascente, Italy's largest department store. He began designing windows, and later became a consultant in the fashion department.

"I always said exactly what I thought," he says, "and that got noticed. You know, in these huge department stores if you want a career there are a thousand compromises you're supposed to make. I didn't, probably because I knew I didn't want a career there. I would go to the person who had sold underwear for twenty years and say, 'Look at this underwear. It's ugly. And I don't accept ugly things.'"

Armani was hired away from La Rinascente by Nino Cerutti, who was looking for an assistant. It was in the Cerutti factory that Armani began working with textiles, and by the late 1960s he was comfortable in his $40,000-a-year job. "I was doing well," says Armani. "I was privileged. I'd go to Paris and London and people knew me. But I couldn't do what I knew I should be doing. There was no real progress."

The turning point for Armani was his meeting Sergio Galeotti in a Forte dei Marmi nightclub. Galeotti, then twenty-five and a draftsman in a Milan architectural firm, persuaded Armani to go out and do it on his own.

"He made me look inside myself," says Armani. "And suddenly I realized that I wanted something more from the world. He convinced me to leave. Only someone as young as Sergio would have pushed me to risk all that without a thought."

Armani began as a consultant for companies like Ungaro and Zegna while Galeotti set up the business end of their new firm. In 1975, with $10,000 and one receptionist, they founded Giorgio Armani SPA, and Armani designed a collection for men. The women's collection was introduced the next season.

"We did in ten years what most people never do in several decades," says Armani. "But in that time there started to grow a kind of sadness in us, a remorse. The sadness was that we knew we were losing what we were ten years ago. We used to laugh—at other people, at ourselves. We used to take off and go to the movies in the afternoon. It took over our personal lives. That's the price of success. If we hadn't done that we wouldn't be where we are now. You have to be very, very hard on yourself, because that's the way the rest of the world is going to be.

"It's so demanding that you can close off the humanity you think you have. I saw it happening. I saw it happening between me and Sergio. Little by little there started to be breaks in the human side of our partnership. We weren't eating together, there was too much work, and when we saw each other we were always working again.

"After we got very successful Sergio began pushing me not to think only about work. He said 'Life is passing. We are not young anymore.'"

This August Galeotti died after a long illness.

Armani threw himself furiously into his work, determined not only to carry on with the upcoming collection but to shoulder Galeotti's business responsibility as well. With his work load already staggering, the designer now estimates he spends three hours every morning overseeing business and financial matters before he even starts to design. "As long as I can I'm going to do it myself," says Armani, who is now in full control,

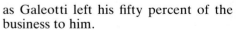

as Galeotti left his fifty percent of the business to him.

He is, he says, better prepared for his new tasks than people might believe. "It simply isn't true that he made deals and I designed. We did that, of course, but then I also designed deals and he dealt designs. We did everything together."

The groundbreaking Armani collection for spring 1986—a collection that proved once and for all that Armani can design as well for night as he does for day—was, in Armani's words, a fulfillment of Galeotti's belief in the design-

"My clothes are modern precisely for the time and place one lives in. Women today live very differently than they did twenty or thirty years ago; their needs are different, and the way fashion is made has to be different. A designer at this moment holds a very important place. He must understand the jump, that little click, that's happened in a woman. My chic allows a woman her sense of interpretation."

Armani's specific formula of dressing the new woman: "a casual putting together of elements, pieces that never make up an ensemble, but have a harmony among themselves."

er's ability to excel at any kind of design. "Doing this evening section was one of the last decisions we made together. He believed I could do evening and he pushed me to do it."

Now Armani seems eager to start projects he and Galeotti had agreed upon. Foremost in his mind is the expansion of the Emporio line, a collection of younger clothes for men and women aged eighteen to thirty that is sold in Emporio boutiques in Italy and in the Armani boutique in New York—a situation he feels is not ideal. "It's too expensive in the States," he says. "We're working on a solution to that."

He is interested in expanding the line to offer a full range of products. "We did some research in Italy and found that Emporio's customers saw the hand of one designer following everything. That's rare in the younger market, where there's no stability. Even a kid with relatively little money likes a stable product. These clothes take four months to produce. They can't follow fads."

Armani says he wants to sell to fewer department stores, open more of his own boutiques ("I don't want to make a collection anymore and see it selected by people who decide what they think is nice in it"), and learn more about running a multinational business.

The expansion of the design studio is also important because of Armani's serious new venture into evening wear, which he describes as "modern haute couture."

"I wanted to do an evening collection that wasn't traditional. We were terrified people would say it was presumptuous for us to try. Haute couture is so narrowly defined. What I tried to do was to forget that and think of another one, an evening that takes a bit

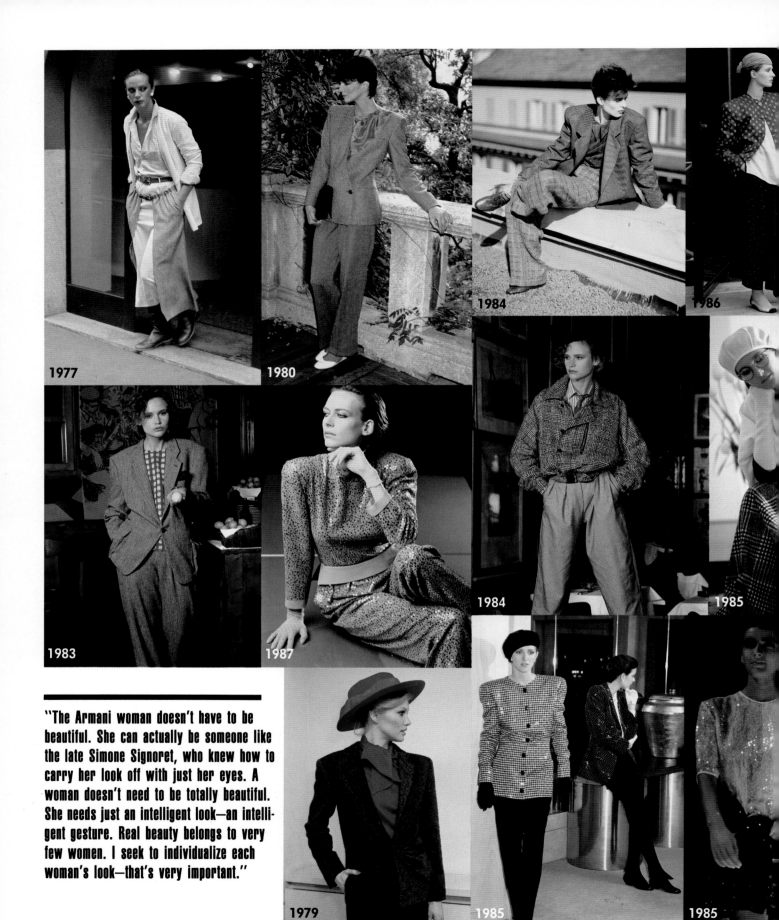

1977

1980

1984

1986

1983

1987

1984

1985

"The Armani woman doesn't have to be beautiful. She can actually be someone like the late Simone Signoret, who knew how to carry her look off with just her eyes. A woman doesn't need to be totally beautiful. She needs just an intelligent look—an intelligent gesture. Real beauty belongs to very few women. I seek to individualize each woman's look—that's very important."

1979

1985

1985

1985

1980

1980

1984

1981

1984

from day and mixes it with evening. I'm sick of huge taffeta and bows for evening. It's OK for a certain woman, but not for every woman. Evening used to be all black gowns. I eliminated black in my collection for night."

Looking back over his years of design, Armani believes, with the rest of the world no doubt, that he has probably made more of a statement with the jacket than anything else.

"I've been making jackets for fifteen years," says Armani. "It's not this sorry, serious thing anymore. I've shown that a jacket can have humor. It's not a blazer, it's a jacket, but it gives you importance, it gives you shoulder, it gives you allure."

When he isn't working, Armani spends much of his time fussing over his various residences—the apartment in the palazzo on Via Borgonuovo, houses in Forte dei Marmi and on the island of Pantelleria. The care he takes with every detail of his austere environs is evident in the details only—overall it looks as clean as pale slate.

"Sergio used to have this joke," according to Gabriella Forte, Armani's American president. "He used to look at all the details Giorgio put so much time into designing around the house and he'd groan and say, 'The designer struck here.' When Sergio got the closets in his apartment he saw the incredible miniature handles that open these wall-sized doors, and he couldn't figure them out. And he said to Giorgio, 'Hey, designer, couldn't we have some of those big round things to open doors, the kind that poor people have?' "

Armani laughs when he hears the story told again, over lunch in his dining room, with the light from the late fall afternoon pouring in.

"I have to be almost violent with myself these days," he says. "I have to recover the vitality that Sergio had so much of. I have to be me and Sergio both, in one. I'm not just speaking of my work when I say that. He knew how to keep in touch with people in a way that maybe I don't. He had such class and elegance. That's something that's still awaiting me, that part of what he did.

"As much as possible," he continues, "I'm going to carry out what plans he had made: to keep our policy of straightforward relations and respect with our clients, to get a little better all the time. You can always improve."

—MILAN, 1985

After a show, 1979

The grand finale, 1985

MAKING THE MOVE

After long months of perfectionist rearranging and reordering of furniture and appliances, Giorgio Armani has finally moved into his new apartment, which is attached to his offices on the Via Borgonuovo. This allows the exacting Armani to keep his eagle eye on everything, and he is known to swoop into the working quarters at the most unexpected moments—a tendency that is facilitated by a secret-passage swinging wall that leads directly from the apartment to the office and is said to be the terror of his staff.

The apartment itself, needless to say, is of the most meticulous minimalism imaginable, with stark white walls and low taupe furniture arranged sparely throughout the two floors. There are, nevertheless, distinct signs of habitation: Giorgio's pure gold shaving brush and toiletries are very artistically arranged in his vast bathroom, and the Armani sweatshirts, T-shirts, and sneakers are beginning to fill his walk-in closet, which is divided by electronic sliding doors. And his long fiber-glass table, illuminated from beneath, was this day discreetly set at one end for dinner.

Armani admits the apartment seems "a little big" sometimes, but he's blissfully happy there, he says, especially since he shares it with Micia, a four-month-old apricot Persian cat, whom allurophile Giorgio is wont to pick up and walk around with as if it were a muff.

—MILAN, 1984

Simple furnishings, "cool" colors

Heading out to sea

The Mediterranean from
Armani's bedroom

ARMANI'S
ISLAND HIDEAWAY

The comma-shaped saltwater pool

The Armani compound

At least three times a year Giorgio Armani touches down on a parched volcanic island in the Mediterranean where the one local dentist keeps office hours one day a week, the warmhearted peasants are just beginning to conquer their fear of the surf, and the largest industry is capers, harvested one by one from the low-lying plants that brighten the brown terraced landscape.

Pantelleria is a craggy, thirty-one-square-mile chunk of often-savage land sixty-eight miles southeast of Sicily and forty miles off the North African coast. It is known to few people outside Italy except avid divers and archeologists who come to inspect ruins of Phoenician towns, remnants of Neolithic temples, and prehistoric caves.

"Once I get here, I tend to stay for several weeks," admits Armani. "In a way, it is a nuisance, but the difficulties of getting here protect its privacy. I am not on Pantelleria for social reasons. I don't know a soul here except for a few local fishermen, market people, the lady who takes care of the house when I'm not here, the people who own the bar in the port, and a local architect. That's just fine with me."

Frustrated, however, by being constantly recognized, the designer was encouraged to move from a less solitary and comparatively chaste dwelling to a veritable getaway compound, masterminded by Milanese architect Gabriella Giuntoli on a steep cliff above the tiny Gadir port for some truly humbling vistas.

As Armani recalls it, the biggest problem posed by converting the centu-

direction.

Despite Armani's protestations that his house is not "luxurious or extravagant," a certain kind of sumptuousness does have the upper hand here, one that puts a premium on serene, uncluttered space. Armani, who worked on the color scheme, describes the cool shades of blue, green, gray, and pink as "those you imagine lying half asleep, half awake on a cool, fresh bed in the half darkness of a bedroom." For Giuntoli

After dinner Armani sometimes rounds up his guests and takes them for a bumpy ride to the port, which is a charming, run-down collection of outdoor cafés so low-key they often don't have names, a single boutique, boat shops, and the Blue Bar, where Armani and his friends like to eat sherbets after dinner. The day ends before 1 A.M. back at the house, over a drink of Armagnac or grappa accompanied by a Tunisian torch song in a candlelit room.

The lacquered luncheon table, set with simple plates and flatware on straw mats

The sleek, open kitchen

ry-old stable and two farmhouses, and building a fourth structure to house a main kitchen and outsized living area, was to retain the indigenous architecture while making the place modern, clean, and comfortable.

Giuntoli, who is involved in urban planning in southern Italy, visited the island for the first time eighteen years ago. "When I arrived there were ugly houses being built out of cinder block and I thought, 'I'm going to forget all about modern architecture and use the local volcanic stone,'" remembers Giuntoli, who has since built twenty houses on the island.

In its most basic form, the Pantellerian abode, or *dammuso*, is a cube of lava blocks with a vaulted roof, a design that evolved in response to an unforgiving sun and powerful winds from every

they are a "restful, refreshing" antidote to the harsh Pantellerian light that penetrates the living room through a clover-shaped skylight.

Life inevitably revolves around the saltwater pool, an emphatic punctuation mark carved out of the expansive iroko wood deck that extends straight through the cantilevered doors into the living room.

Armani's Milan cook is usually in tow, preparing breakfast plates of prosciutto and figs, grown on the property, and later in the day platters of langoustines, red mullet, swordfish, salpa, luvari, oysters, or lobsters. Although Armani likes the brisk, high-alcohol wines made from the local Zibbibo grapes, they lull him to sleep, so he passes them up in favor of "enjoying my house and the island to the fullest."

"If you want discos, cocktail parties, and funny business in the bushes, for God's sake, don't come to Pantelleria," Armani once told a reporter, "it will bore you to death."

—Pantelleria, ITALY, 1984

Armani serves up lunch on the terrace

ARMANI ON TOUR

EYE That Gorgeous Giorgio Armani sure knows how to win customers and influence retailers. From the moment he arrived those California ladies went gaga over him—pursuing him for autographs, feeding him compliments, and one BP even played kneesies with him. What a display. GG loved every minute of it.

Now it's not easy to lure GG away from his Milan palazzo, but I. Magnin managed to snag him for a four-day trip to San Francisco and Beverly Hills, where the store was opening the newest and biggest Armani boutique. The store really put GG through his paces, but that dear boy has such stamina, he smiled through it all. In San Francisco he greeted and charmed more than two hundred of the store's best customers who came for cocktails and a mini-version of the fall show GG did in Milan.

Things were different in Los Angeles, on a grander scale—seven hundred invited for a cocktail buffet and show in the Dorothy Chandler Pavilion at the Music Center, a $50-a-head benefit for KCET, the public television station. It was a grand effort, but Perfectionist Armani was not terribly pleased with the results. "The room was too big for this kind of show," he said when it was over.

But it wasn't all business for GG and his gang. Magnin's took them away from it all for a day in the Napa Valley: a tour of Sterling Vineyards; lunch at Ardath and Claude Rouas's stunning restaurant, Auberge du Soleil; and a swim and dinner at Richard Tam's fantasy house. GG was won over by it all. "Though we've been very busy, the whole trip seems more like a holiday."

—SAN FRANCISCO, 1981

Clockwise from top left: A vineyard gondola; the San Francisco show; GG with Marisa Berenson . . . and Rosemarie Stack; GG relaxes; touring wine country

CALVIN KLEIN
The Boy Next Door

When Calvin Klein began his meteoric rise in 1973 he was just thirty years old and people were still asking, "Are you Anne Klein's son?" (The answer is no.) Now, with his sophisticated, gimmick-free sportswear, he has established himself as the foremost exponent of spare, all-American style. But, as he has said, "It's important not to confuse simplicity with uninteresting," so he imbues his collections with the rich crispness or sensuous slouch of natural fabrics and never forgets the body underneath.

But Clean-Cut Cal also knows when to stir a little excitement into his clothes. When he peddled his denims on television the commercials were banned by some stations, but Klein was soon selling 400,000 pair a week. Next, he crossed the gender barrier with women's underwear fashioned, in a brilliantly commercial masterstroke, after traditional men's underwear. And the launch of his Obsession fragrance was one of the most successful ever.

In very lucrative partnership with his childhood friend Barry Schwartz (Klein Enterprises paid them each $12,047,000 in 1984), Klein enjoys the trappings of prosperity. In September 1986, Klein married Kelly Rector in a surprise ceremony in Cernobbio, Italy. It is one of life's sweeter ironies that if he had yielded early on to Schwartz's urging, the two would have been in the supermarket business today.

WHAT MAKES

The first pea coat, 1971

Calvin Klein moves restlessly on the U-shaped brown suede sofa in the starkly modern Upper East Side apartment he shares with his wife, Jayne, their six-year-old daughter, Marci, and a huge sheepdog named Snoopy.

"My image is that I'm young, eager, and kind of sensitive," explains Calvin, who fits the bill with his cropped hair, tennis sweater, and anxious-to-please charm. "But I've just had a very traumatic birthday—I turned thirty.

"Five years ago, I knew exactly what I wanted—to have my coat-and-suit business. I did it with my school friend, Barry Schwartz, and his ten thousand dollars. We've surpassed all our expectations. We are constantly refusing takeover offers from public companies. Now the big question we face is just how far do we want to expand?"

Jayne sprawls beside Calvin on the sofa, wearing a red Sonia Rykiel pantsuit she bought in Paris, then gets up to fix a Scotch and water for him and a ginger ale for herself.

"We retail coats and suits from about one hundred forty to one hundred sixty dollars," Calvin continues. "Last

year our volume was four million dollars; this year we expect it to be five million."

Jayne returns with the drinks, and Calvin immediately picks up her ginger ale and drinks it. "That's exactly what he's like," she says. "When he's talking about business he's unconscious of anything that's going on around him."

At present, expansion plans include taking over another floor at 205 West 39th Street, the one vacated by Dan Millstein, Calvin's first employer when he graduated from the Fashion Institute of Technology. "Negotiating with Dan to take over his showroom when his company went out of business was one of the hardest things I've ever done. When I first called him, Dan didn't want to talk to me, and our relationship got so bad that finally I had to leave everything to Barry."

Ironically, Calvin believes that a major reason for his own company's success is that so many coat and suit manufacturers have disappeared from the scene. "We have very little competition, and that's what makes it easy for us. So many people today say there is no coat business. My God, there's plenty of it around. I wouldn't mind more competition—it makes me work better."

Calvin and Barry went into the "contemporary" price range in 1967, he says, because they saw a void in the market. "There has always been a couture level of clothes, which I always thought

was kind of dead. The level beneath couture interested me—clothes that are good-looking but also young, clothes that Jayne and her friends would wear. Five years ago the market was largely ignored; even fewer manufacturers are in it now."

Calvin met Jayne when they were both students at F.I.T., where Jayne trained as a textile designer. "And we'd lived most of our lives in the same Bronx neighborhood, so it was practically a girl-marries-boy-next-door story.

"Jayne is constantly in my mind when I design. She is our kind of customer. She grew out of wearing junior clothes five or six years ago. She wanted something better. But she certainly wouldn't buy clothes on a couture level. They're too old and too expensive for her. Our kind of customer just doesn't believe in spending that kind of money on clothes. They're not that important to her. She'll spend it on travel or decorating, but not on clothes. She likes to look 'today,' but she doesn't want to spend all day worrying about what she will wear at night. She's very secure about herself and her clothes."

Calvin reckons that his major hangup is that he "eats, sleeps, and drinks the fashion business. "It's really true that if you're going to be successful you have to work at it hard. I'm completely disorganized about everything except my business. My job is my hobby as well as my work. At night when I'm home I'll sit

Calvin with Jayne, 1972

CALVIN RUN?

Crossing the gender barrier, 1983

down to relax, then maybe do a hundred sketches."

Calvin is in the office by eight each morning and leaves about seven. "In the beginning it was seven days a week in the shop, and often twenty-four hours a day. Barry and I would ship until three in the morning and then sleep on the convertible sofa in the showroom. There isn't any job in the place I haven't done—and I'm really proud of it."

His dedication has reaped them financial rewards, but Calvin insists he has no status symbols: "So I drive a Mercedes—the engine knocks and the garageman keeps telling me I should get it fixed—and I've started collecting some things—lithographs, posters. But there is not one thing that I own that would upset me greatly if I lost it. And I don't intend to keep any of these things the rest of my life. I want to constantly change things. If I had everything I wanted, it would be a bore."

Calvin regrets that he doesn't spend some more time, however, on himself. "I should exercise—some mornings my back kills me, just bending over to brush my teeth—but I just don't have the patience. Two years ago I joined a gym. I was so exhausted the evening I went that I took a cab from my office on Thirty-ninth Street to Thirty-fourth Street. I paid the two hundred dollars, but I never went back."

Asked about today's mood in fashion, Calvin says his favorite French couturier is Yves Saint Laurent, because "he is the only one who's in touch with young people.

"But there are really no leaders in fashion today—no one really can dictate what fashion will be from season to season. It's not good or bad, it's just what's happening. The customer doesn't care how talented or friendly a designer is—if his clothes don't work for her, she won't buy them."

Calvin sees big changes taking place in retailing: "If department stores are going to keep up with the times, they will have to change their coat, suit, and dress departments to 'resource departments.' Everything I have to offer, coat or dress, should be sold in the same department. If I put two good dresses in a collection and they're bought by the dress department, they got lost; but if they are sold along with my other clothes, they get snapped up."

But Jayne has the last word. "Barry sums up Calvin's attitude to business this way," she says. " 'He's the easiest man in the world to get along with, as long as he gets exactly what he wants.' "

• •

By the end of the fiscal year in May 1975, Calvin Klein and Barry Schwartz, his best friend since childhood, will have grossed $12 million as partners in Calvin Klein, Ltd., one of the most successful ready-to-wear businesses on Seventh Avenue. In a time when many businesses are closing or cutting back, Calvin Klein, Ltd., is expanding. The first Calvin Klein boutique is tentatively scheduled to open in March at Bloomingdale's; almost simultaneously, Tokyo's Isetan will open another, and Kaufmann's, in Pittsburgh, will follow in June. "We will have at least a dozen shops open by fall; it's just a question of choosing who we want in each city," says Schwartz.

The ramifications of this growth seem endless. "We can easily see this becoming a thirty-million-dollar business in the next three to five years," continues Schwartz. "And that's only ready-to-wear," chimes in Klein. "I'm already doing a fur collection, and although I've played around with men's wear and tested it once, successfully, with Saks, we're now thinking about it seriously."

Then there's licensing. "We made our own accessories this season, but I don't want to be in the handbag business, or the fur business," he says. "Even though it allows me more freedom when I do it myself, there are good licensees." Klein rattles off some of the possibilities: shoes, belts, scarves, hats. The one thing he resists is perfume. "Unless you're in the hands of one of the two giants, who will advertise and promote, it just isn't worth it. I don't want to get involved in something that doesn't have a chance. And I don't need it for a living. Licensing is just meant to complement what we're doing."

Other changes are in the works as well. In order to expand distribution, yet service the 400 stores the firm now has (narrowed down from 1,700 in 1971, with a goal of 300), they're about to turn the firm over to computerization. "At our level we could probably sneak by without it now, but we will be more efficient with it," says Schwartz. "The firm has gotten too big to control manually."

The division of labor is simple at the

Talking about his Obsession, 1986

top. "It's beautiful," says Klein, "because Barry absolutely runs this business. I devote my time to fabrics, design, anything involved with the collection. Barry takes care of the showroom, sales, production, shipping, publicity."

"I get all my satisfaction out of the bottom line—making money for this company. That's my function here," says Schwartz, the one of the pair who organized their selling ice water when they were five (five cents a cup) and newspapers when they were eight (Barry bought them for three cents and sold them for seven).

"But I also realize the taste Barry's developed," says Klein, "and many times use him as a sounding board for design. We discuss everything."

Explains Schwartz, "We talk between eight and nine in the morning, then at the end of the day and weekends, if necessary."

It's a lot different from the days when Klein wheeled the first collection up to Bonwit Teller himself, on a wobbly dress rack missing one wheel, so nothing would get wrinkled.

Seven years ago, after the High School of Art and Design and F.I.T., Klein was designing junior suits and coats for Dan Millstein. Schwartz, after high school and New York University, was running the family business, a supermarket on 119th Street in Harlem, which he left, putting up $10,000 to join and finance Klein on Seventh Avenue. It was the first and final financing the company has ever needed.

They opened a small showroom in the York Hotel on Seventh Avenue in April 1968. As to what really put them in business, Klein emphatically states: "Mildred Custin [then president of Bonwit Teller] and my understanding of what people really want to wear. Miss Custin believed in what I had to say."

"And she backed it with dollars: exactly fifty thousand dollars on the first order for about a thousand pieces," says Schwartz. "And it wasn't just clothes. They ran an ad every month for the first year in business and we didn't contribute a thing [to the cost of the ads]." The one thing Miss Custin insisted was that they raise their prices. "She said we couldn't make our clothes profitably the way we had them priced, and she was right." They went up immediately, from $49.75 to $65.75 (wholesale).

"So it really wasn't any one particular style that built our business," says

1979

1980

1984

1985

1985

1987

1986

1982

1982

1982

1982

1984

1981

CALVIN KLEIN 171

Klein. The company has, however, made history with the pea coat. "Everyone here wonders what version I'm going to do next because each year it has been different." The first one Klein did was for fall '70 at $59.75, and the firm sold 20,000. The second, at $65.75, sold 30,000, as did this year's version at $69.75. "I'll have to do something for next fall," says Klein, "not because I have to, but because I want to. That's the reason I went into this business: so I'll never have to do anything I don't want to.

"We don't want ulcers, over a store, for example," he continues. "We'd rather drop an account than have too many problems. And no store has ever asked me to make or do or change anything. I do it my way. If they want it, I'm happy; if they don't, fine. All I ask is that they be honest."

"We're not limited financially from doing anything in the world Calvin wants to do," says Schwartz. "For example, we stopped emphasizing coats and went into sportswear because Calvin said that's the way people were living and that's what he wanted to do."

Klein doesn't see as many of his customers as do his saleswomen, who each season take three duplicate collections around the country for trunk shows. The two men visit management at stores in other cities, "but now Calvin only does major charity events, such as the symphony show in Kansas City," says Schwartz. "Maybe seven or eight a year."

"I can remember one year when I was on the road the whole month of September and was sick when I got back," says Klein. "But I need the give-and-take I get from customers. A woman in Chicago bought a dress that was supposed to be full, immediately called the fitter, had it taken in two inches, and put a belt on it. She thought I would be insulted, but it was sensational."

Klein engulfs himself in his work, and has been known to lock himself up in the design room for six days without seeing the sun. But, as it was put when Klein was introduced for his return Coty Award (his first was the year before), this team of thirty-two-year-olds is busy living "The American Dream." Says Klein, "That's why it's so much fun."

But two distinctly different people are living it. Klein is always on the go. In the past year he covered Paris, Scotland, Rome, Frankfurt for fabrics, Egypt on

With partner Barry Schwartz, 1975

After the Fall 1981 show

vacation, Rio, and the West Coast twice—once over Christmas with his daughter, Marci, who he says "is reality for me." Klein is divorced, living in Manhattan, and soon to move into a spacious East Side apartment. Klein often goes out for business lunches and dinners. If it's not business, he's with friends at theater openings and parties, although not as much as he'd like. "And this year I'm into bodies and health," he adds, looking forward to continuing his interest in riding, tennis, and gym.

Schwartz is less gregarious. Married, with two children, he goes home after work. He hates the city, lives in suburban New Rochelle, where he can be around animals and tend his gardens, and is looking for a farm in Maine. He vacationed in East Africa last summer, has an office of photos to prove it, and will return this year.

"The secret to our success is all the clichés," says Klein. "Hard work and a desire to do something honest. And before we're partners, we're best friends. Nothing can come between that."

"We're lucky," says Schwartz. "When we were kids we wanted to go

into business together. Calvin had everything in his house that ever walked. We both wanted to open a pet store."

Backstage before the show there was an uncanny calm. There were Calvin Klein, his design staff, hairdressers, makeup artists, dressers, and an unprecedented number of mannequins—seventy-two of them—and yet the usual pandemonium surrounding a big Seventh Avenue opening was more like organized enthusiasm.

But once Klein's 113-piece collection for fall 1981 hit the runway, the excitement began to generate, and at the finale retailers and press were claiming that this was Klein's most important and best collection to date.

Klein himself wasn't even aware of the impact he had made. "There were certain parts of the collection I was really very pleased with," says Klein, "and this was the first time I recall seeing such smiles on the mannequins after they showed their outfits. You could tell they felt good in the clothes and they felt the

audience reacting to them. But it wasn't until I read the reviews the next day that I fully realized the strength of the collection. I was in a state of shock."

Klein had spent at least six months building this four-star collection, selecting the fabrics and colors, designing the prints, and ultimately creating the shapes. "The biggest challenge," says Klein, "was doing lots of color for fall. That's the most difficult area, but once

Stretch jeans, 1979

"I've tried over the past eighteen years to develop a style, a certain way of dressing that a woman expects from me—purity, line, cut, a modern way of dressing, whether it's a dress or jacket and pants. Within that framework I change the cut, the silhouette, the color, the length, the proportion, but still retain the Calvin Klein signature."

the fabrics started coming in I was thrilled. And the other part of the collection that pleased me was the dresses. I knew the coats were good, because coats are easy for me to design, and I've been involved with sportswear for so long. But it was the dresses that intrigued me. After the show Sonja Caproni of I. Magnin said the dresses were as comfortable as sportswear. As I had worked on them, I had seen that was happening, and I became very excited.

"There's no question about it," Klein continues, "this was the best reaction ever to any of my collections. But the ultimate acknowledgment is still to come. I wait until the customers acknowledge it by buying it. It's their review I'm waiting for."

Still, Klein says, "The sense of fulfillment is tremendous. I've had all kinds of success. But if a designer is truly dreaming of being acknowledged, this was the collection that did it for me."

It was the collection that did it for the retailers, too, who had been waiting for a Calvin Klein blockbuster after a few seasons of good-but-not-terribly-new collections.

Even with a few so-so seasons, Klein and partner Barry Schwartz have managed to build an impressive empire. Schwartz estimates that total retail sales for all Klein products will top $600 million this year—$400 million produced by Puritan Fashions, which manufactures men's, women's, and children's CK jeans; $60 million from Klein's own ready-to-wear company; $20 million from cosmetics; $5 million each from belts, patterns, sheets, and scarves.

The CK collection is also produced in Japan under a licensing agreement with Isetan department stores in Tokyo, and an agreement has been signed to cover Brazil, although all the legal complications have not been resolved. In addition, there is a Calvin Klein boutique in Browns in London, another is expected to open in Milan this year, followed by one in Geneva, and Schwartz expects to open stores in South America soon.

In reflecting, Klein adds, "The thing about success is enjoying it. After this show Barry said, 'Just really enjoy it. You've worked hard for it.'

"At first I thought of taking off for several months. But I feel wonderful," continues an elated Klein. "I don't want to think about a vacation. I want to get right back to work."

—NEW YORK, 1973, 1975, 1981

1984

1978

1986

1981

1982

1985

YOU'RE SIXTEEN, YOU'RE BEAUTIFUL, AND YOU'RE KLEIN

Marci and Dad

The white grand pianos

Friends of ... the birthday girl

The chalk-faced waiters

It was the *Gone With the Wind* of Sweet Sixteen parties—a pull-out-all-the-stops production that would have exceeded the most ambitious fantasies of Marjorie Morningstar's mother. Father Calvin Klein had celebrated his bar mitzvah nearly thirty years before at his parents' house in the Bronx; his ex-wife, Jayne, recalled thinking that her own sixteenth birthday fête in the Hawaiian Lounge of a big Manhattan hotel was the last word in glamor. But their daughter, Marci, came of kissable age amid a slick, circus-sized extravaganza of a party at Studio 54. "I wanted to give her a party she'd remember all her life," said Papa Calvin. There is little doubt she will.

The evening began at 8:30 with 220 of Marci's friends invited for a sit-down dinner. They walked through an entranceway straight out of Busby Berkeley—seven white grand pianos in a diagonal line on a black Plexiglas floor; seven sleek female pianists in white tie playing "That Old Black Magic" under hanging baskets of white English coun-

try roses. They then proceeded through a walkway of six-foot red birthday candles, for which innumerable real little birthday candles were melted down, to brush through an autumn-leaf carpeting of seventy thousand pastel birthday bows, to seat themselves on banquettes wrapped up to look like giant birthday packages.

They came from prep schools from North Carolina to Connecticut, from private schools in Manhattan. They talked in that concentrated, intense manner peculiar to older adolescents. Some of the boys mistook Calvin Klein's date, Bianca Jagger, for a fellow pupil.

Many of them said that they came to Studio 54 every Friday, and that they loved getting dressed up. "It's the new classicism," explained Carter Cooper, the seventeen-year-old son of Gloria Vanderbilt and the late Wyatt Cooper. "It used to be chic to be sloppy; now to look put-together seems important."

And then there was Marci—a gracious if slightly bewildered-looking center of attention, as the crowd multiplied with 770 postprandial guests, ranging from rocker Mick Jagger to socialite Judy Peabody. Marci was handily the most sophisticatedly dressed female there, in a short white jacket and black pants from her father's upcoming spring collection, an outfit her father says she at first resisted "because she thought it made her look like a waiter."

Sometime after midnight, the mirrored Mylar walls parted to reveal a steep glass staircase on which thirty female dancers in black-tie drag did a *"Chorus Line"*-style march down the stairs. Two men in tails led Marci up the staircase, where her father waited for her with a candled cake, while about a thousand people sang, "Happy birthday, dear Marci." The confetti fell, the balloons floated overhead, the fireworks went off in tumbleweeds of silver, and everyone danced.

"Everyone's asking how much it cost," said a cheerful Calvin Klein the following morning, "but it was just a matter of some confetti, some balloons, and renting a few pianos for the evening."
                                    —NEW YORK, 1982

Calvin and Jayne Klein with Bianca Jagger (*center*)

HOT CALVIN

San Franciscans are a hardy lot who seem to thrive on nonstop partying. That's the way it was for five days of fêting and feasting with Calvin Klein. The occasion? I. Magnin invited Klein, who hadn't made a personal appearance outside New York in five years, to bring his fall collection for a show to benefit the San Francisco Ballet Auxiliary. Klein arrived sans staff four days ahead to select and fit models, rehearse, pick the music, and do endless interviews and TV shows. In between, Magnin's managed to sandwich in enough parties to keep Calvin on the move, and there's no doubt that San Francisco thought that Calvin was Hot.

The luncheon-fashion show was billed as "An Elegant Affair with Calvin Klein," and several women were certainly open to the idea of an affair, elegant or otherwise. Hot Calvin's age of elegance is paying off. And it's paying off at retail, too. "We did over sixty thousand dollars with the women's collection in the first three days of selling after the show," said I. Magnin vice-president Sonja Caproni.
—SAN FRANCISCO, 1982

Out for a sail

Hot, Hotter, Hottest Calvin backstage with Carmella Scaggs

AT HOME WITH THE FGS

It was billed as a private Studio 54 reopening party honoring the former Studio impresario Steve Rubell. And while hundreds stormed the Studio gates as eagerly as Frenchmen once stormed the Bastille, the *real* party to be at was Calvin Klein's select gathering at his Sovereign apartment.

There were the Hollywooders rubbing shoulders with the Fashion Glamor Set and a few dozen of New York's most beautiful models. The BP group was led by the Ambassador to the Court of the Ladies, Jerry Zipkin, who had Nan Kempner on one arm and Patti Davis on the other. Heading up the pop-rock contingent was Deborah Harry, with her natural brown hair. The prettiest star of the evening was Brooke Shields, escorted by the FGS host, who rarely left her side.

"It was the best club we ever had," said old Studio regular Halston. "It was a sociological phenomenon. It was always a club for everyone, and I know it will be just great again."
—NEW YORK, 1981

Shields and Jack Nicholson

Deborah Harry

Brooke Shields, the party host, and Christopher Reeve

Jerry Zipkin and Diana Vreeland

Dick Cavett and Mary Tyler Moore

Halston and Marina Schiano

Calvin Klein on Career Chic . . .

A career woman has devoted time to the work she loves. She's busy, and she needs the kind of clothes that work many different ways. She's got to work it so she can take three jackets, or three sweaters, and wear them with four important blouses, and then put them together with two skirts or three pairs of pants.

Beyond those specifics, "The woman has to look as if she weren't studying a magazine—she's got to have her own style. She wants to give the impression she's working, not that she's a fashion freak.

"The woman in a position of authority and power has to have a sense of quality," he says emphatically. "A sense of quality and style separates her from the rest of the bunch—a cashmere sweater instead of wool, a silk crêpe de Chine blouse instead of polyester."

As for the specifics of the Klein Career Chic wardrobe:

SKIRTS: "one dressy in silk, one in flannel or garbardine, one in suede or leather."

JACKETS: "three of them—tweed, cashmere (like a sweater), and one in leather or suede."

PANTS: "very skinny jeans, pleated trousers, and a flat pair in twill or flannel."

SWEATERS: "one has to be cashmere."

DRESSES: "one in silk, mostly for after dinner."

"Any of these pieces could mix with anything else," says Klein, "providing, of course, that the colors are neutral, with bright accents in the accessories. But an absolute *must* is a cream silk blouse." Another of Klein's "musts" is a fur. Why? "For warmth, for glamor, and to make a very definite impression about who she is."

1986

1986

1980

. . . and on Packing It In

Summer or winter, Calvin Klein's favorite vacations are to the sun. His five-minute formula works the same way each time. Into a huge, well-worn khaki Hunting World bag go lots of T-shirts, a cashmere sweater, white pants, denim jeans, red jeans (for color), sneakers, sandals, toiletries, and a little cassette machine.

He says it's important to fit all your travel clothes into one bag. ("If it doesn't go on the plane with me, it doesn't go. I hate to wait for luggage or take the chance it will get lost.")

His suggestions for women on the go:
• Lay out the clothes and accessories you plan to take so that you can pare them down easily.
• Pack underwear in scarves that can be stuffed into corners.
• Put shoes in separate plastic bags and tuck into corners.
• Separate clothes with plastic dry cleaner bags or tissue paper to prevent wrinkles; roll soft, large pieces of clothing in plastic like a sausage.
• Sachet smells divine.
• Keep jewelry and accessories to a minimum.

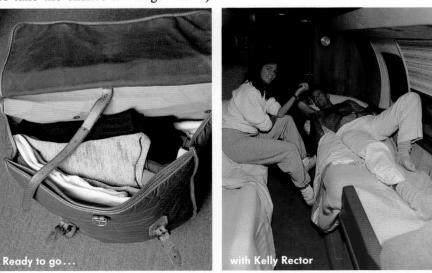

Ready to go . . .

with Kelly Rector

The Battle of Tokyo

By the time they reached Japan, the hostility between the two had escalated, and Oscar de la Renta had shed all inhibitions about badmouthing Calvin Klein.

"If one of my girls came out in a dress that was a broom and one of his girls came out dressed in gold, my girl would make mincemeat out of his girl," Oscar sniffed.

It is a strange, indecipherable quarrel, having as much to do with selling dresses in Tokyo as any real or imagined slight Oscar may have suffered. Japan, after all, is worth contention: American designers with Japanese licensees will have sales of about $150 million this year. And compared with Europeans, who have been in Japan longer, that, as they say, is peanuts.

But the Americans are gaining. Klein, whose royalty agreement is with Isetan—Japan's answer to Bloomingdale's—claims to do $25 million. De la Renta, whose clothes are manufactured and sold by Japan's oldest department store, Mitsukoshi, claims a volume of $50 million.

Each of the designers lays claim to being better known than the other. But common knowledge has it that Oscar is Number One, with Isetan investing millions of dollars—including a $750,000 print campaign and a $500,000 fashion show—in making Klein as well known as the Imperial Sun King.

Which leads one to suspect that Oscar, who by his own admission is a very competitive guy, may be motivated by greed and envy. Oscar, of course, denies this. The source of his angst, then?

"Calvin never returned my phone calls."

It began the previous spring, as Oscar remembers, when fate (and Japanese market week) brought the two together. "When I heard that we were both going to Japan, I said, 'Gee, how wonderful. We could pool our resources and we could each bring more girls and each girl could make more money.'"

Calvin, however, has an entirely different philosophy on sharing models:

"I always use my own girls. It is part of my identity. When you start seeing the same models in everybody's shows, the clothes start looking like everybody else's."

In any case, Oscar called Calvin. He called him three times. When he didn't hear from him, negotiations began between the designers' assistants. At issue were models Pat Cleveland and Alva Chin. Oscar booked them first—for a fashion show on Wednesday—but agreed to release them for Calvin's earlier show on Monday.

The courtesy, however, was not returned. Says Oscar's administrative assistant, Jack Alexander, "We were insulted. Not only didn't they want us to use Alva and Pat, whom we had booked first, but when I went to book one of their models, I was told Calvin had booked her for Tuesday, the day she was flying home."

Needless to say, rumors abounded. With so many models involved—Calvin was taking thirty-six, including twelve men; Oscar, nine—there had to be gossip.

One well-circulated story accused Oscar of trying to stick Calvin with Alva's and Pat's airfare. Another accused Calvin of pressuring the girls not to work for Oscar. Still another intimated that Calvin was cheap. Several models, the story goes, passed up Calvin's fee of $1,700 for four days' work, thinking they could make more money in New York. (Oscar was paying his models $3,500 for seven days.) Calvin insists he did return Oscar's calls—twice—but Oscar was on vacation.

No matter, says Oscar, suddenly turned philosopher. "Success should make people behave wonderfully."

Calvin Klein is behaving like a fashion impresario. With a week to flight time, his assistant is working out the logistics of getting scores of people to the airport. Not only is Calvin taking all his favorite mannequins—mostly Vogue-types like Christie Brinkley and Patti Hansen—but for his very first fashion show in Japan, his entire crew will be there, including his favorite soundman (Ray Yates), his favorite hairdresser (Christiaan), makeup artist (Ariella), personal photographer (Arthur Elgort) and photographer's assistant.

"The point of this is to show American design on American girls in an American show," says Calvin.

To further that aim, he rejected all but two Japanese mannequins and saw to it that the Oriental ornaments on the walls of the New Ohtani ballroom—where he is holding his shows—were covered with simple white drapery.

Oscar, on the other hand, seems less concerned with images of Americana. On this, his eighth trip to Japan, he and wife Francoise invited Brando Brandolini and Louise Melhado to partake in that side of the trip in which Oscar seems to revel.

"I love things Japanese," he says. "I love Sumo—that's Japanese wrestling. It's a passion of mine. I once traveled 14 hours just to see a Sumo match. Sumo champions are culture heroes there. Not like fashion designers who might be stars, but real heroes, almost gods."

And so they arrive. Calvin on a Friday. Oscar on a Saturday. Various model contingents in between. Right from the beginning, there are contrasts: Calvin greeted by flashbulbs and a Toyota, Oscar by flowers and Pontiac limousines.

Oscar is jovial, expansive, bitchy. "Is Calvin here yet?" he asks. When told that he is, and that he is both showing and staying at the New Ohtani, Oscar laughs. "That's like coming to New York and having a fashion show at the Hilton."

Calvin, as usual, is perfectly organized and meticulous. He greets his models with pizza and Dom Perignon. He signs autographs for the salesgirls at Isetan.

Oscar's trip, meanwhile, is taking on farcical overtones. Yes, he is working with Mitsukoshi store executives—the first of his three fashion shows at the Imperial Hotel is not until Wednesday—but every spare minute, it seems, is taken up with Sumo.

An infatuation has begun. Sumo champion Takanohana has done the unheard of. He asks Oscar, Francoise, Brandolini and Melhado to dinner. The fare is steak tartare and the talk is mostly Japanese.

Brandolini keeps asking, "Who is this Calvin Klein?"

Calvin's P.M. show: a subtle spectacle for 600 guests. Calvin is a whirling dervish. He kisses. He cajoles. He whispers and applauds. As is his custom, he handles every detail himself.

The response, though, is anti-climactic. At the end of 50 minutes, the applause is mostly from the models and staff. Store executives point out that applause is not a Japanese custom. The best-known guest is Ambassador Mike

Signing autographs

Mansfield and his wife, who just that afternoon lunched with Francoise and Oscar.

Calvin commits the unpardonable: He embraces his mannequins on stage. The Japanese find this barbaric. The next day's paper comments. So does Oscar:

"I was told that his show was boring, that nothing worked—the music, the clothes. One dress of mine fills a whole stage. Calvin needs forty or fifty dresses to make it look like something."

Oscar's black-tie, $150-a-plate dinner show for 1,000 is a sellout. In attendance are the Mansfields, the ambassador of the Dominican Republic, Prince Takeda and some cousins of the Royal Family. Mitsukoshi president Shigeru Okada (whose daughter is married to Prince Takeda's brother) flies in from Peking for the event.

Here, too, the audience is reserved. The crowd, as one observer puts it, reacts more in a manner of saluting a friend than cheering a celebrity.

Klein's exposure in Tokyo is unprecedented in the annals of Japanese media hype. Four newspapers carry stories of his arrival. There is a 60-minute feature of his life on Japan's version of "The Tonight Show," "Eleven, PM." All the TV news shows carry features on his fashion show. He is interviewed by five magazines. He appears on two TV talk shows. He holds a press conference for 200 newspaper reporters.

"Our publicity has a lot more depth than Oscar's," says Akiko Sugimoto, a fashion coordinator for Isetan. "Oscar's posters just announce his name. We tell people about Calvin and his lifestyle."

Sales the day after Calvin's shows are up 80 percent, according to Isetan executives. No one knows for certain, though, if the week's steady increase in Klein sales is due to a physical renovation of the Klein boutique or to all this publicity.

Calvin shows heroic stamina. In seven days, not one cross word about Oscar. He leaves Tokyo on a flight to California. Oscar, meanwhile, deserts to Kyoto for more fashion shows, more Sumo.

—NEW YORK/TOKYO, 1979

He is French fashion's most complex contradiction—a designer who made his name with macho-flavored bikers' leathers, and yet has the finesse of a real couturier. Whether he's designing absurdist wing-shouldered jackets or a simple tailored gabardine jacket, Claude Montana is guaranteed to bring to it an eye for proportion, cut, and detail that is unrivaled among today's young designers. "I don't believe in people who do one collection and they are a hit," says Montana. "One has to pass through a lot before it becomes good. You need time to know your possibilities." When he manages to temper his predilection for operatic fantasy—a tendency he acquired during a teenage stint as an extra with the Paris Opera— he has very little to worry about. His real-life clothes, executed in strong silhouettes and touched with a sense of low-key drama, are among the best Paris has to offer. A shy man who is never without his protective camouflage of tough-guy padded-shoulder jackets and tight jeans, Montana says he has few moments when he's not thinking about his work. "Two weeks in the sun, not thinking about my work, is something that is not possible for me."

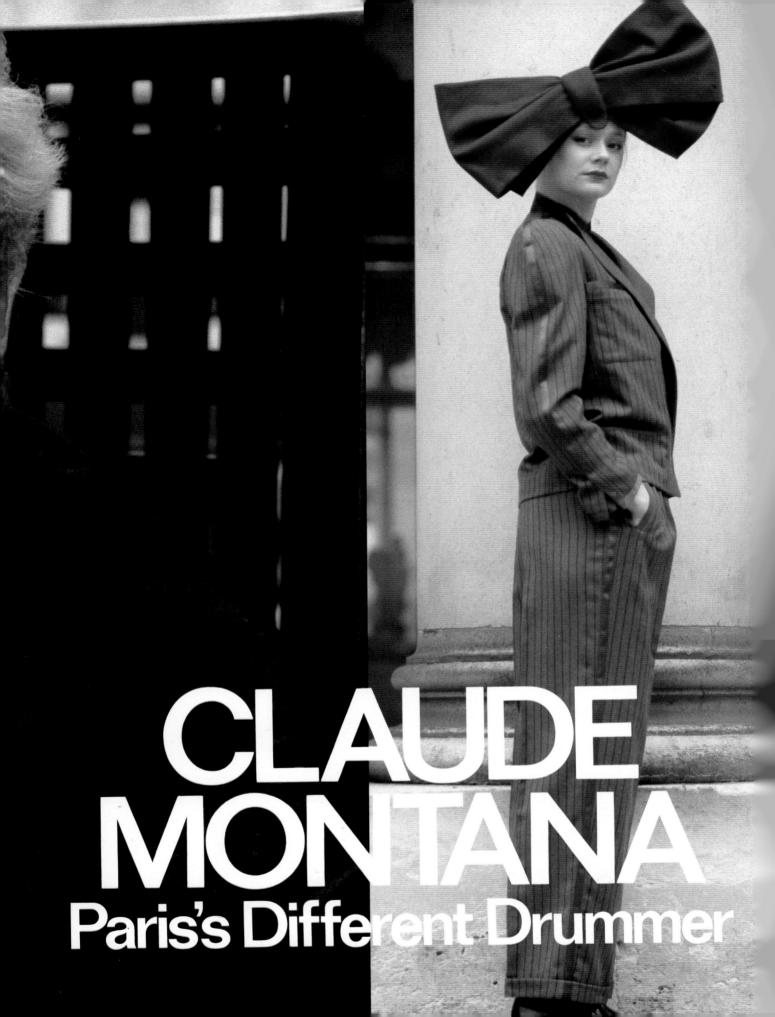

CLAUDE MONTANA
Paris's Different Drummer

By his own admission, Claude Montana is a bundle of inconsistencies. His slight body and fair skin look absurdly out of place in the "uniform" he has worn since about 1969. His scraggly blond hair and soft, at times lilting voice belie an iron character that knows how to get what it wants and has withstood a barrage of biting personal criticism. And the elaborate clothes that made him famous as one of Paris's most avant-garde designers indicate little of his quiet, almost common lifestyle. Even his name, which most people assume must be fake, conjures up contradictory images of a comfortable French bourgeois businessman alongside a rugged biker.

The plain truth is the name is genuine (coming from his Spanish-born father), and his personality contains few of the characteristics normally associated with either kind. He is more like an intelligent, thorough schoolboy, who has uncontrollable fits of wild genius and a rather eccentric adoration of anything American, especially its lowlife.

He grew up in Paris, where his father was a small fabric manufacturer and his mother a housewife. Although neither parent was French (his mother was born in Germany), they both came to Paris at an early age and became thoroughly "French," at least in their ambitions for their three children.

The first son and daughter met their expectations, but the youngest, Claude, never quite did. He went to high school, did well, and then after receiving his degree fled Paris and bummed around Europe for a few years, finally ending up in a cold-water flat in one of London's seamier neighborhoods.

"My brother became the research director of a huge chemical company, and my father wanted exactly the same kind of life for me," recalls Montana, who perfected his English during his brief London sojourn in the early 1970s. "I didn't know what I wanted, but I knew it wasn't that. I left Paris because I couldn't stand my father's disappointment."

But even cold-water flats cost money, and Montana and a friend started making papier-mâché jewelry out of

CLAUDE REIGNS

A Landmark Collection

1981

1984

What was wrong with Claude Montana? The air backstage after the showing of his fall 1984 collection was dense with superlatives. The more rhapsodically inclined were fanning themselves out of fashion faints, cold-cash-conscious retailers were actually grinning, and Montana looked miserable.

The designer of what people were calling "the collection of the season" had tucked himself into a corner closet, where, if you were able to find your way there, you'd have seen him receiving congratulations with the ashen, abstracted look of a prisoner saying good-bye before he walked the last mile.

A month later, the memory of his moment of triumph can still produce an unsettling shiver in the thirty-five-year-old designer. "When the show is over, it's like an earthquake that runs through your whole body," he says. "You're split between the idea of running out of the tent and staying, but hidden, just to see who's come backstage to see you." The response this season reassured him, but only for a moment.

"Each season there's this whole thing you have to deal with: In the city of Paris, maybe eighty designers are going to show collections, and out of that people are going to remember only four or five. You try to put it into your head that you can't be at the top for the rest of your life. But for me it's not an easy idea."

It is an index of the designer's relative ease with his métier today that in this collection he played down the spectacle in favor of a new, clean-lined elegance. The strong silhouette was still there, but the self-consciously themed effects and exaggerated, often campy accessories had disappeared. "I'm now trying to do clothes people can relate to, something a woman would really think she could wear. It's the natural way for a designer to develop."

Certainly, for retailers the collection marked a coming of age for the former enfant terrible. "It puts him in a whole other league," says Ellin Saltzman of Saks Fifth Avenue. "Now his clothes look sensational on the stage and on people's backs. He's a creative genius, and I don't use the words loosely."

Says Kal Ruttenstein of Bloomingdale's, "It's time for his business to explode. We see him as a world-class designer." (And a great favorite as well: Style-loving vandals have shattered windows at Bloomingdale's to steal the merchandise displayed there three times.)

All this praise translates into big volume for Montana, whose empire, including licensees, took in a volume of about $35 million in 1983. This sort of popular acceptance—plus the fact that the label makers are calling Montana the heir apparent to Yves Saint Laurent as the King of French Fashion—should allow Montana to relax for a moment. Not at all, says the designer. "I have this kind of anguish, that as soon as one collection's over I have to know exactly what I'm going to do next." —PARIS, 1984

1987

1979

1986

1978

1985

1986

1985

1980

1982

1983

1982

1986

1984

1986

1986

1987

1980

"I think that to others the name Montana means leather, but then people have a tendency to cling to one idea in order to categorize things. For me, fashion is the emotions and experiences of the past six months transformed into each collection, but I try to keep a common thread so that the collections are not disjointed. Sometimes the ideas do not work out, but I hope that the bad helps the good to exist. I would like to think I am true to myself and to my ideas."

stores to place orders. "We made just enough to put a few more shillings in the electric meter," says Montana. Then there was trouble over working papers, and Montana came home.

He became an assistant designer at MacDouglas, the leather fashion house, simply because there was an opening and Montana had nothing better to do. He discovered his love for—and talent with—leather, still always a major part of his collection, and within a year he was chief designer. He also started to experiment with other materials, and by 1974 was designing free-lance for several small clothing companies.

"I knew absolutely nothing about making clothes," stresses Montana, who still seems a little surprised by all that followed. "I didn't know how to cut patterns. But I learned, and I had some ability. It just seemed to work." In 1975 he teamed up with a Spanish knitwear and fabric manufacturer, Ferrar y Sentis, which was looking for a younger image, and he started to work under his own name. At the same time, he hooked up with Beatrice Paul, his genial but shrewd business manager, who also became friend, confidante, and travel companion.

There was controversy and talk from the beginning: Montana was regarded as either a fashion genius who could make dramatic, inspired clothes or a con artist who had no technical skills and fostered a perverse image of women. There was no middle ground. His manner of dressing and his shy, retiring manner, even while dancing away into the wee morning hours in some of Paris's wilder discos, only increased the gossip and fueled the curiosity.

Still, he had begun to get favorable press coverage, and boutiques in Paris and Japan started to buy his clothes. ("The Japanese weren't all that sure they liked it, but they didn't want to miss out on anything," he explains.) And American stores started to become interested. They complained about late deliveries and the prices, but they still bought.

"I was misunderstood for a very, very long time," concedes Montana, who still resents the bad publicity he received in 1977, when he showed what were called "Nazi-like" motorcycle hats and chain accessories. "It was just a catchy thing to say, and it ignored the other things I showed, like spencer jackets and full trousers."

But in fall 1978 Montana scored a major success with his lively sailor linen looks, pinstriped slim skirts and tunics, and double-breasted jackets. And with the collection that followed, Montana received almost universal acclaim for his wide-shouldered coats, peplumed shapes, and embroidered taffeta jackets. It was a great runway show that had buyers and press out of their seats yelling bravo.

In between, Montana had switched backers, largely because Ferrar, as a Spanish company, had trouble importing fabrics into the Common Market and was not right, according to Montana, "for producing an entire look from day to night." He teamed up with fabric producer Gibo for clothing and Ballanti for knitwear.

"I was misunderstood for a very, very long time."

Montana and his twelve assistants have moved into a spacious new atelier on the Rue St. Denis, the heart of Paris's red-light district. His business has grown, but his newfound wealth hasn't affected his personal life all that much. He still has no hobbies—other than collecting records—and he lives in the same functional apartment he bought from Nina Ricci designer Gerard Pipart several years ago, complete with Pipart's leftover furniture. The only obvious Montana touches are the extraordinary stereo system, whose several walled-in speakers make the place throb like a disco, his Sonia Delaunay sketches, and a living-room floor full of window-high plants.

His only luxuries are a daily visit to a local gym and several brief vacations each year in the U.S. and Capri. He spent a month this summer traveling around Hawaii, California, and New York, and he tries to get to America at least four times a year. Along the way, he usually gets a good dose of the more bizarre night and morning clubs, which he finds irresistible, and by the time he gets back to Paris similar places pale by comparison. "They don't have the same atmosphere, the same mix, or even the same music," says Montana, who used to be seen almost every morning around three at one of the bars on the Rue St. Anne or a leather joint on the Left Bank called the Manhattan, where even his outfit is considered quite classic.

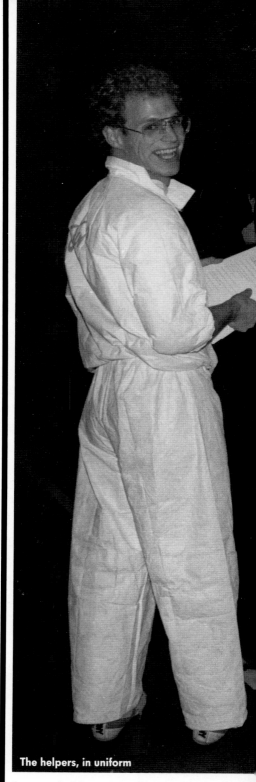

The helpers, in uniform

It was fashion groupie-watching at its best. The main event, of course, was Bergdorf Goodman's show of Claude Montana's fall collection (to benefit the Grey Art Gallery and Study Center of New York University), complete with all the extravagances—including thirty-five models—typical of a Montana Paris production. An unexpected addition was the opener: the whirling appearance

EYE

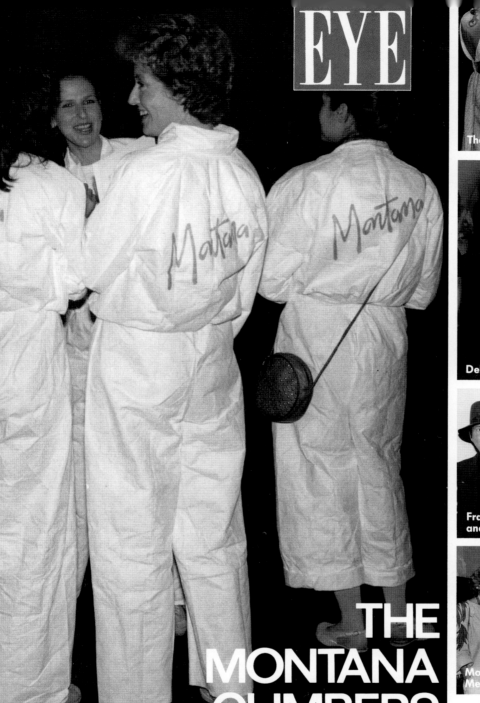

The finale

Deborah Harry

Mary McFadden

Francesco Scavullo and Cornelia Guest

Montana with BG's Dawn Mello and Ira Neimark

Leathered fans

THE MONTANA CLIMBERS

of a female impersonator.

And off the runway there was another show going on. There, the leathered, broad-shouldered set grossly outnumbered the tame and safe. Most in evidence were exaggerated makeup, electrified hair—Blondie's Deborah Harry's was a neon orange—and short skirts, including the several thigh-high sweatshirted Norma Kamali versions that passed through the white-tunneled entrance.

Bergdorf president Ira Neimark thought that, despite the Seventh Regiment Armory's cavernous environment, complete with bleachers for the fans, there was a "feeling of intimacy." That was certainly true of the Glorious Foods–catered dinner following the show.

As starched Marine Corps guards stood erect and security types manned a set of closed doors set rocking on their hinges by the crowd, a select forty-seven squeezed through the barrier to the Clark Room and shared oysters and caviar, rack of lamb, and raspberry-filled figs with the designer. What really put a gleam in Montana's weary eyes was Bergdorf's "show of appreciation": a pair of spurs. "You really know what I like," said the designer as he studied his gift.   —NEW YORK, 1981

1985

"I'm not designing for a special woman but for a woman who likes to wear my clothes."

baked toilet paper and fake rhinestones at home. The jewelry caught the attention of an editor at British *Vogue*, who splashed them all over the magazine and persuaded a few of the trendier English

An upcoming show for about one thousand guests at Bergdorf Goodman in New York is in many ways a sign to Montana that he has made it, that mainstream stores and clients will now seriously consider buying a Montana dress or coat. But he is very careful not to become too mainstream, an established figure for whom younger designers will feel the same kind of dislike (not contempt—he is too soft-spoken for that) he himself has for most of Paris's older couturiers. In fact, the only other designer for whom he feels "real admiration" is Mme. Gres, whom he has never met, but who he thinks "does the only real things that will last and are eternal."

Montana has also stopped dabbling with the idea of moving to America, which he finds the most exciting place in the world. "Anything is possible there," he says. "Style and craziness combine, and there aren't the cobwebs to get in your way." But he recognizes that "for the kind of work I do, America is not really the right place. I'm not mainstream enough, and if I were an American designer I would be a failure. But this way, across the sea, I'm something exotic and different. I think I'll try to keep it that way." —PARIS, 1979

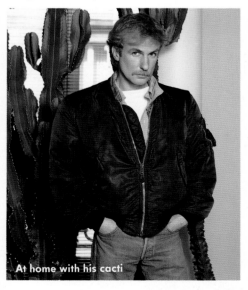

At home with his cacti

CLAUDE MONTANA 191

When Donna Karan closed the collections on Seventh Avenue in May 1985 with her premiere collection under her own name, she brought down the house. The personal appearance tour that followed broke sales records, and the success of Karan's fledgling company has catapulted her to the forefront of the American design community.

It was an achievement that delighted everyone and surprised no one. A college dropout bent on a design career, Karan had worked her way up to becoming sportswear pioneer Anne Klein's associate designer. When Klein died in 1974, Karan took over as chief designer and brought the fashion community to its feet her first time out.

Working with her associate, Louis Dell'Olio, Karan carried on the Anne Klein tradition with uncomplicated separates that gave classic sporty looks a stylish edge: great blazers, clean-cut pants, bold coats, sarong skirts, and dresses cut with the ease of a T-shirt. And the team added a key ingredient to the Klein formula: Tough Chic, expressed in such turnouts as hacking jackets with short black leather skirts.

On her own, Karan mixes her taste for the tailored with a body consciousness that is consummately feminine.

DONNA
KARAN
New York's
Rising Star

1985: HER FIRST DONNA KARANS

The SA collections ended on a high note: Donna Karan presented a collection that was New York fashion at its most sophisticated. It was hard to find a buyer in the Karan showroom who didn't love the collection, and the designer was treated to a long, standing ovation.

With its subtle big-city sophistication, many form-following shapes, and some high-ticket items, "this is a collection that has to be nurtured," said one Fifth Avenue retailer. "It's going to be hard to sell it, but it's going to be worth it."

And what was the word once the customers saw it?

"The people who came in were buying entire wardrobes," says Sydney Bachman, vice-president and fashion director of New York's Bergdorf Goodman, which generated $200,000 in sales in the three days the collection was sold from samples—a month before stock was due. "They weren't buying a top, a bottom, or an outfit."

In California, Karan's easy, almost girl-next-door attitude, coupled with her comfortable clothes, captivated retailers and consumers. She set records at I. Magnin in San Francisco and Saks in Beverly Hills for one-day sales of a designer sportswear collection: Each store did in excess of $100,000.

Magnin's Sonja Caproni said women were buying interchangeable pieces that would give them several outfits. "These are designer customers, and originally we thought it would be for only tall people, but we have sold in all size ranges."

Saks customers saw an evening fashion show and came to the store the next day to buy. Patty Fox, the store's fashion director, said, "Our customers want ease and comfort in addition to travelability and quality. On top of that they got a name."

—NEW YORK, 1985

PRIMA DONNA

When she was growing up on Long Island, the kids at school nicknamed her "Popeye" and "Spaghetti Legs." Except for softball, volleyball, and basketball, there wasn't much doing at school that interested her. Her mother was a career woman on Seventh Avenue, and when she came home from work she was usually too tired to pay much attention to her daughter. In short, no matter where she was, Donna Karan just didn't fit in.

"I was a social misfit, and I wasn't very accepted," she says, recalling two painful memories from her childhood. In one, a seven-year-old Donna stepped up to bat, pulled back—and smacked her best friend across the nose, breaking it. In another, a "gawky, flat-chested" Donna stuffed her bathing suit with toilet paper—only to forget and jump into the water.

"I didn't go out, I didn't socialize, so I had to find something that I was good at doing," says considerably more confident Karan today.

There was, after all, her passion for clothes and for working in boutiques after school. And one day in Hewlett High, she dreamed up her first collection, using her body to trace the patterns since she didn't know how to make the real thing. As awkward or out of touch as she might have felt then, she hit on one thing she was good at—designing clothes—and it has stood her in good stead ever since.

Assistant to the late Anne Klein when she was barely out of her teens, Karan today sits at the head of one of the most ballyhooed and eagerly anticipated new lines to come down Seventh Avenue in ages—Donna Karan New York. With a controlled first-year distribution of about 125 stores, her new company is projected to do $11 million its first year—and may break even.

"That's not even supposed to happen," says a breathless Karan, reeling in the attention and excitement that has surrounded her since the collection was shown two months ago.

"I'm still scared, and I don't un-

The designer at home in her Upper East Side apartment

derstand it all," she says of the line's initial success. "I just wanted a few friends to wear it," she says, shrugging back into the self-effacing Karan, a persona that alternates at lightning speed with the confident, brash young woman who tends to talk in the dulcet tones of a carnival barker.

Speaking with her today, there is no evidence of the gawky, quiet teenager who skipped classes to hang out in the art department at school and who longed for her mother's attention. The shy child is gone, replaced by a bubbling, exuberant woman who talks in shrieks of happiness or dismay. Not for her the subtle entrance and exit. At the end of her last Anne Klein collection with former co-designer Louis Dell'Olio, Karan sobbed and bawled on the runway like an out-of-control kid.

Today she is making clothes for the perfectly poised woman of the Eighties—all muscle-toned chic with slim hips, strong shoulders, and buttocks that are packaged neatly in the curve-defining scarf skirts she made a critical part of her premiere collection. It's a special look that retailers say is one of the most innovative American collections in years.

With its center of gravity based on the bodysuit—until now not a very intriguing piece of fashion outside of exercise class—Karan has pared down a

woman's wardrobe, offering her the ultimate "packable" separates that can be wrapped, tied, switched, and swapped using only a few basic essentials. Black is the pivotal color. Despite the practicality of the idea, there is another, completely impractical aspect to the collection—her clothes have some of the highest price tags on Seventh Avenue, with a gold sequined blouse retailing for about $1,900. Still, Karan contends that there are pieces, such as the wool jersey skirt for about $90 retail, that will make her collection accessible to many women. And as she explains it, "Your whole closet shouldn't be full of expensive clothes. Great pizza is still great pizza."

Karan settles down in her eclectically furnished living room, full of contemporary furniture, some antique chairs, and sculpture by her husband, Stephan Weiss, to reflect on the phenomenon that has surrounded her these last several months. With her bare feet, big white shirt, and pulled-back hair, she looks more like a Fifties teenager than the head of an explosive new company. Her emotions flicker from confidence to utter bemusement as she runs down the events of the recent past. "I found it totally shocking that the customer actually likes it."

The collection was, in many ways, a real departure for Karan, who owns 50 percent of her firm. (Takihyo, Inc., the Japanese firm that backs Anne Klein, owns 30 percent, while Tomio Taki, that firm's head, holds 10 percent and Frank Mori, president of the Anne Klein Group, owns the other 10 percent.) This effort marks not only a new beginning, but the end of a ten-year design partnership at Anne Klein with Louis Dell'Olio, her friend since they were students together at Parsons School of Design.

"I'm starting from scratch and aiming at a different customer from that of Anne Klein," says Karan, zeroing in on her design concept. "I want to completely dress a woman in the best of everything."

Karan says she sees her customer "as I see myself—a woman who doesn't have time to shop, a mother, a traveler, perhaps a company owner. I will design only clothes and accessories that I myself

Karan after her first solo Anne Klein show

1974: HER FIRST ANNE KLEINS

An excited, appreciative audience filled the hour of Donna Karan's first solo Anne Klein collection with almost non-stop applause for every skirt, jacket, and evening gown that graced the runway.

"We don't need one other collection. It's the greatest group of clothes I have seen in my twenty years of retailing," said Bill McElree of I. Magnin. Said John Schumacher, the store's president, "We'll buy lots here. This was the most paralyzing collection I've ever seen."

Saks Fifth Avenue concurred. "It was fantastic," commented Rae Crespin. "Absolute perfection in sportswear." Added Henry Callahan: "Every piece was like a jewel."
—NEW YORK, 1974

1979

The Anne Klein Years

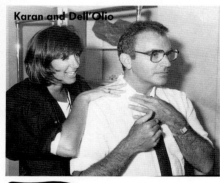
Karan and Dell'Olio

Donna aimed at a more personalized collection," Louis Dell'Olio explains, looking at their ten-year Anne Klein collaboration. "Evening clothes, for example, reflected what she would wear at night." One of Dell'Olio's functions was to expand the look to meet a larger Anne Klein audience.

Historically, the look of Anne Klein mirrored a marriage of both designers' moods each season. "People who know us always guessed about which number was whose idea. And they were always wrong. Our personality differences were not reflected in the clothes.

"It is our differences," he continues, "that will prevent Donna's collection and mine from overlapping. Donna's collection will be much smaller, but more diversified, and will have a price range that goes both higher and lower than Anne Klein's."

Says Karan, "I'm starting all over, while Louis has this fabulous organization behind him. But I knew someday I'd go on my own, so I never wanted my name on another's label."

She is taken by surprise when asked if she foresees even the possibility of a professional reunion with Dell'Olio. "Who knows? Steve was my first love, whom I returned to years after the split with my first husband; I went back to Anne Klein nine months after she had fired me. My whole life has gone that way."

—NEW YORK, 1984

1981

1985

1985

1985

1982

1984

1984

Karan at home and (*above*) with husband Stephan Weiss

would wear. The Anne Klein customer is more varied than that. Louis can meet her needs."

When it is suggested that the inseparables might be vying for a similar market, Dell'Olio has said he doesn't feel competitive with Karan. "And," he added, "I don't feel it with Calvin or Ralph either. We all have our niches."

"I'm attached to, and proud of, Anne Klein," says Karan, who will continue to act as a consultant. "You can't imagine how much I want Louis to succeed." She concedes that two designers for one company can be "a weakness—more expenses, two points of view, less focus." Yet, she says, the decision to break the partnership was painful. Her enthusiasm for her new venture mingles with sadness as she anticipates "the loneliness of not being able to yell 'Hey, Lou. . . .' "

Despite the tentativeness, Karan is a woman with seemingly limitless goals, and she is not shy about voicing them: She wants to open her own boutiques, particularly in Europe; she'd like to do men's and children's wear; and, although it requires a tremendous amount of work, she's plenty interested in that hallmark of designer licensing, the fragrance business. "I have a plan that's all worked out. I've just got to hold back so I don't blow it," she says, her cockiness intact once again.

Fresh from the multi-million-dollar success of Anne Klein II, Karan is eager to start her own lower-priced line, keep-

ing the Donna Karan collection a select, expensive "laboratory" of fashion where she can test her ideas. This, of course, doesn't even touch on the ancillary businesses she entered when she started the new company—hosiery, bodywear, and accessories, from jewelry to belts and hats.

Karan is the embodiment of all that is New York—fast, loud, bright, funny, egotistical, demanding, and generous. A self-confessed suburban girl "from one of the Five Towns" on Long Island, she

realized a long time ago that she wanted the comforts and trappings that many of her contemporaries had. For while she grew up in a wealthy community, hers was not a cushy life. Her mother sent her off to camp at age three and a half so she could pursue her career as a model and saleswoman, and her father—a custom tailor who, she says, "made suits for gangsters"—died at about that same time.

"I've worked since I was fourteen years old," she says. "I loved clothes and I loved retailing." After a less than brilliant career in high school, Karan edged into Parsons "on trial," and tried to land a job with Anne Klein as a sketcher.

"When I met her, she said, 'Let's see how you walk.' I thought, 'So what does walking have to do with sketching?' But I walked and she said I'd never make it as a model. When she finally looked at my portfolio, she hired me—I was a great pin-picker-upper—and stayed nine months before I was fired." The reason, she says, was "I tried so hard I couldn't get anything right. 'There's nothing you can do for me here right now' is how she put it. It was the biggest blow of my life."

For the next year and a half, Karan worked under Patti Cappalli at Addenda, "learning and growing. I thought I wanted to prove that Anne Klein had made a mistake. No, let me change that. I wanted to prove I could make it. I

PRESIDENTIAL MATERIAL

EYE This is the most wonderful day of my life," said Donna Karan in typically ardent style at the October 1985 White House State dinner for Lee Kuan Yew, the Prime Minister of Singapore. "She's warm, she's statuesque, she's elegant," said Karan about Nancy Reagan. Karan looked pretty good herself, dressed in one of her own gold lamé sarong skirts and lots of gold jewelry. She was seated at the head table, next to Warren E. Buffett, the Omaha-based financial wiz whom Nancy Reagan invited to the dinner after being seated next to him at Kay Graham's party in her honor on Martha's Vineyard.

called Anne and asked to come back. I know what I want and go for it."

Shortly after her return to the company, Karan became Klein's associate designer. "I was traveling to Europe, conceptualizing fabrics, working seven days a week and nights. Louis had gone to Teal Traina after school. When I was pregnant and Anne became ill, I asked him to join me." The first group she created as associate designer was "mostly suede and leather—including fringed skirts, stencil cowhide separates, and black Lurex sweater dresses."

In 1974, days after the birth of her daughter, Karan's mentor died, and she found herself the twenty-six-year-old fledgling designer for Takihyo. "Now I look at the Anne Klein company and know it will continue, because it's so strong; at that moment it was a question," she says.

But if Anne Klein was a great sportswear designer, she was just as great a teacher: Karan's first solo collection, in May 1974, made her an overnight sensation. "I almost wished the collection hadn't gone so well," she mused at that time. "What if I can't do it again?" But, of course, she has—consistently.

Single-mindedness has brought her the highs she has experienced in her career, but it has, Karan confesses, also left her with some black holes in her life. Today, when her daughter Gaby, who is now eleven, comes home with a problem in her lessons, Karan admits she finds it hard to help her.

"Stephan and I are both visual people. I'm not a reader, and it's hard for me to retain written information. It's a one-dimensional kind of life. Sometimes I even feel dumb," she says, revealing a long-harbored desire to go back to school at New York University for a degree in liberal arts.

Karan, married to Weiss for the last two years, says he was her "first love" before she married her ex-husband, Mark. After that marriage dissolved, she went after Weiss with the same determination she uses in attacking her career. Today they live an extended-family life in a three-bedroom apartment-studio on the Upper East Side with her daughter, his son or daughter (they alternate living there), a housekeeper, and two cats.

Despite the frantic activity that makes up her life, Karan says she tries to be the attentive mother to Gaby that she

INVESTING BY DESIGN

Designers are very emotional people. I help them direct their emotions in the right direction," says Tomio Taki, the guiding force of Takihyo Co., Ltd., sole owner of Takihyo, Inc., the U.S. firm that provides 100 percent of Donna Karan New York's financial backing. Taki says he looks for qualities that portend "a long creative life." He turns away people who "look at the market first," and encourages those who "design what they believe in."

For Karan, he approved a $3 million backing. "The initial buck starts with him," Karan observes. "I mean, we're talking it's his money. But he never questions anything I do.

"If I, or any of us, should go off the deep end, God forbid, he figures we'll learn from our mistakes. I asked to be CEO of my company and he said OK. Every day is an experience," she continues, laughing. "But I'm learning. If I need him

Tomio Taki

he's always there."

Taki says he approved capitalizing Donna Karan as a separate company because both she and Louis Dell'Olio were "ready and capable to do their own vision. I figured, why not capitalize on what I have in the company? I have two very unique talents. I can make two very unique businesses out of this."

craved growing up. "Until the day I die I will be a guilty mother," she says, confessing that she tends to spoil Gaby because she is not home with her often.

A tomboy when she was growing up, Karan says it is women who fascinate her today. "Now I think women are more interesting. They're doing so many exciting things, they're confused, and they don't have role models. We need tips about other things besides diapers and formula," she says.

Her own confusion about her career led her to attend an est seminar on the "Power of Being" as she contemplated breaking off from Anne Klein.

"It helps you to be clear about life," she explains. "It's as though somebody opened a window. 'Power of Being' is what creation is all about. I felt so disorganized with work and with myself."

But the person who has had the single most dramatic impact on her life is her husband, whose name she invokes with devoted fervor during her conversation. A sculptor who also owns a family company that produces sets for Broadway, Weiss was instrumental in

slowing the workaholic Karan down to a screeching 80 mph. It was he who made her realize that her work was just that—work—and that there was more to life to enjoy, such as art, their families, and the time they can spend at their rented house at Water Island in New York. Now she even talks enthusiastically about having a baby.

He was the one to take charge of her newly developing company, helping his wife shape it in her role as chief executive officer and a partner. For although she had been at Anne Klein as chief designer for ten years, she was still an employee there. Now she has to worry about budgets and overhead.

"While Donna was crying, Stephan was the one pulling it all together," she admits, in frank admiration. And although he helped establish the company and could continue to have a role there, Karan is afraid her two-year-old marriage to him would suffer.

"Fashion is great and it's exciting for me, but relationships are what it's all about," says Karan.

—NEW YORK, 1974, 1984, 1985

1987

1986

1985

"This is a time marked by speed and energy," says Donna Karan. "Clothes have to be relaxed with an element of drama. My whole collection is based on options and flexibility."

1986

1986

If, as the title of a novel once put it, blessed are the debonair, then Bill Blass was bound to be one of the most fortunate of that singular species. In his sixties, the silver-tipped New York designer retains the perfect carriage, impeccable manners, and martini-dry wit that have made him a favorite on the Manhattan social circuit, almost from the day he arrived from Indiana. Blass, photographed here with a group of BB-clad loyalists in 1979, has always known his customer, so a Blass collection always has something for everyone; he knows just how to cut camel hair coats, flannel trousers, and terrific coat-dresses, but he is also happy to please the woman who likes her evening wear to show every dollar she's invested, giving her dresses that are sequinned and beaded to a fare-thee-well. He swears his heart is in the country—Connecticut, to be exact—but this quintessentially sophisticated man has developed an urbane image appealing enough to build a multi-million-dollar name that has shown up on everything from chocolates to cars.

BILL BLASS
The Last of the Movie Stars

1985

1985

BLASS APPEAL

None of his friends in Fort Wayne, Indiana could understand why eight-year-old William Ralph Blass chose to draw the things he did. While other children presented sweetly acceptable sketches of houses and pets, little Bill came up with detailed renderings of cocktail shakers, Manhattan penthouses, men in dinner jackets, and women in white fox coats.

That this child in the dead center of middle-class America at the height of the Great Depression should create a fantasy world straight out of Cole Porter or Ernst Lubitsch seems today uncannily prescient. Bill Blass, who was born in 1922, represents the quintessence of urban sophistication to millions of people. He lives in a penthouse on East 57th Street, he wears a dinner jacket with more ease than any other man in town,

and he designs for—and often is seen in the company of —just the sort of women who would have worn white fox had they lived fifty years ago.

Blass himself doesn't perceive the metamorphosis from hometown Indiana boy to millionaire designer and bon vivant as surprising. "I don't think coming from Indiana has much to do with anything," he says in an even, low-pitched voice that suggests a gentrified Clark Gable with a touch of an English accent. "Norell came from Noblesville, Indiana; Cole Porter, Mainbocher, Hoagy Carmichael—they all came from the Midwest. They had a sense of what they wanted to do; that helps more than anything, I think. I know I did."

That confidence has sustained Blass very nicely. Success didn't come early to him, but when it did, it came in torrents. Today he stands as the sole head of an empire that encompasses about three

dozen licenses bearing the Bill Blass label and takes in over $200 million, with a personal income for Blass of an estimated $3 million. He occupies four floors at 550 Seventh Avenue. His lavish, only-for-the-affluent ready-to-wear line—while a comparatively minor source of Blass's income—has given him stellar visibility. They are clothes with their own distinctive nimbus, a compound of snob appeal and an amusing sense of the sheer joy of dressing up.

"The ultimate role of clothes is to please the individual," says Blass, "not to keep one warm or cool. Nothing gives people a greater sense of pleasure than knowing they look better in what they have on than anything else."

This sybaritic philosophy of dress was shaped, in large part, in the flickering half dark of Fort Wayne's movie theaters on Saturday afternoons in the Thirties, while an enchanted Blass di-

"My point of view is totally American. I like to think it's clean-cut, crisp, modern, wearable, and pretty. My clothes are, most importantly, actually meant to be worn by women. The idea of fashion just as an amusement or part of the theater of a fashion show is totally ridiculous. You have to know when and how women are going to wear the clothes you design."

1967

gested endless images from the films "portraying a very sophisticated way of life.

"Every Saturday afternoon with Garbo, Dietrich, Lombard dressed to the nines. My God, think of those clothes. Movies really gave me my background in fashion."

The son of a hardware-store owner who committed suicide when Blass was five, Blass says he had decided to become a designer by the time he was six or seven. "Fashion had a glamor, a kind of excitement that had nothing to do with the environment I was in," says Blass. "I seemed to be passing time, just waiting." He went through the perfunctory motions of the life expected of him—joining the high school football team, sketching for the school paper—and began selling sketches of dresses to Seventh Avenue by the time he was fifteen, for $25 or $30 apiece. He graduated from high school and took a train

"I couldn't wait until I was old enough to come to New York, but I didn't show my impatience. I didn't act as if I was dissatisfied with where I was, and that's been partly true of my career. I did not have an early success, but I waited."

straight to the place he'd always intended to go, New York.

"I remember friends of the family asking why I wasn't going to the art school in Chicago. That's not at all what I was looking for. If you're going to pursue something, you have to be in New York. Somewhere around Pittsburgh, I had some doubts, but never after that."

In fact, Blass's slow, forty-year ascendancy to his present status seems to have been remarkably free of doubts or regrets. As he takes inventory of the various phases of his career—his first job as a sketcher at nineteen, a detour of three and a half years with the army in World War II, gradual stages of apprenticeship at the firms of Anna Miller and Maurice Rentner—he says the only thing he wishes he'd done differently was to have worked for a couture house in Paris early on. ("I wish I'd learned more of my craft from that standpoint.")

"A lot of what happened to me had

BB on the Business of Fashion

I know it sounds perfectly ridiculous," says Bill Blass, "but I often dream about clothes." He also works on his collections at the opera and the ballet. "I do not have a great ear for music, and my mind wanders. Seeing something on the stage that has nothing to do with everyday life enhances the creative process. It starts the juices flowing."

Although he says there are times when fashion design can be called art, he considers his work to be a craft. He cites the work of Balenciaga, Mme. Grès, and "instances of Yves Saint Laurent" as art, "but I don't consider myself one of them," he says.

Blass likens his craft to that of a painter or a writer. "Each time one designs a collection, I suspect it's a little like a painter or an author starting a manuscript. Although you want to continue your own style, you want a fresh approach each time."

His occupation, says Blass, is not a solitary one. "Much of it is done on the run. I find that external interruptions are stimulating. The thing that stimulates me most is when I'm fitting a collection I will have twenty phone calls, and people walking in and out from production, from selling, from publicity, all asking me questions.

"Some designers lock themselves up," Blass continues. "I don't work that way. If I attempt to sit down and say, 'OK, I have to do five black short dresses by Thursday,' I can't do it. But then I will be someplace and see something there that will trigger inspiration."

Among the places Blass finds most inspiring are museums. "I've been to almost all the great museums in the world."

Once an idea surfaces, Blass sketches it on a small scrap of paper. His initial drawings are, for the most part, doll-size. "I have sketch pads

The Dress of the Season: Fall 1982

here and there," Blass says, "and I'm always drawing. I sketch while I'm talking on the telephone, while I'm in a car, while I'm on a plane. I sketch dresses, shoes, hats, anything and everything that might be appealing as a silhouette."

Blass then enlarges the sketches that he thinks are "valid" for a collection. He matches the drawing to the appropriate fabric, sampled earlier,

> "God knows, I've had some seasons when I wasn't particularly hot. But in my old age I've been rediscovered, and when it happens to you, you've got to grab it."

and then hands it over to one of his assistants and steps away. "I don't oversee them as they're being worked on. They're not interesting to me at that stage. They're like children when they're toddling. They're not interesting until they get up and walk. I leave them alone until the first fitting."

He files away any sketches not put into his upcoming collection for possible future use. "I've had sketches that I've held back three, maybe four, maybe five seasons and then brought them out and had a bestseller. Timing is important. It's a happy combination of the right fabric in the right style at the right time that makes a successful dress."

What quantifies the success of a dress for Blass? Not the critical acclaim, but "how many backs it actually got on."   —NEW YORK, 1985

to do with luck, but an awful lot with patience—sitting back, accepting what comes your way, and digesting it. There are lots of designers younger than myself who are no longer visible because they don't have that patience. If you want something badly enough, you get it, in time."

Being a designer on Seventh Avenue in the Forties and Fifties provided an exacting test of patience. "At that time, designers were kept very much in the back room, almost something to be ashamed of. The minute a collection was over, we were encouraged to take long holidays, which gave the manufacturer a

chance to totally change the collection." At Maurice Rentner, where Blass had worked since the firm merged with Anna Miller, he became increasingly visible, swiftly amassing a heady following of socialites and celebrities, many of whom remain his customers. In 1970 he acquired complete control of the company

1980

1985

1-2-3, the Barberry Room.... Society then was built on being out and being seen. I often wonder how the hell I was able to afford it."

His social propinquity—in both New York and Paris, where he'd go to see the couture showings in the Fifties—gave Blass a chance to observe the type of woman who eventually would become his customer and to formulate his notions of American style. He remembers watching Gloria Vanderbilt and C. Z.

1986

Guest at the Ritz Hotel in Paris.

"It was years ago, when Dior ruled the fashion world with the *tailleur* and those hats. Well, Gloria would show up with a white shirt, gray flannel pants, and a sable coat, and C. Z. would be in a twin sweater set, tweed skirt, and flat shoes—both of them looking like a million bucks. There were the French women, extraordinary in their big hats and padded hips, and two American women who were better dressed than the overly jeweled, overly dressed Parisians."

Blass's admiration for the American woman of style has been more than

from his partners, Eugene Lewin and Herman Seigenfeld, and the ever-expanding empire of Bill Blass, Ltd., began to assume its powerful form.

Blass says he's found many more pleasures than pains in taking sole command of his operations. "The business part—which wasn't easy to learn—has become almost as fascinating as the creative end of it—the juggling, the maneuvering."

Still, Blass hardly has been the work-obsessed Calvinist at any point in his life. If half of Blass's dream was to become a successful designer, the other—and probably equally potent—half was to inhabit the world he saw in movies as a child. From the beginning, he seems to have slid into that world with suave facility.

"I knew a few people when I came here," he says casually. Whoever they were, they must have provided smooth conduits to café society. Blass recalls his youth in New York as a blur of evenings spent at a series of clubs whose names he reels off like memorized poetry. "There were nightclubs of every description. I'd go to the Stork Club or Morocco, Larue,

1984

BB on BB

ON DECORATING: "It has got to be a place that you can absolutely fall apart in. I'm a firm believer that if you have a house, you can do anything you want in it (such as putting your feet on the furniture). I like a certain amount of neatness, but I don't think there should ever be a room where you can't put a book down without destroying the atmosphere."

ON SHOPPING FOR ANTIQUES, which he likes to do with friends: "I always say, in case of shopping with Oscar [de la Renta], I should have twenty minutes' time in the shop before him. He's a ferocious shopper, you know."

ON HIS COLLECTIONS, which spend some time in his apartment and then are unceremoniously retired to a downstairs storeroom as he buys new ones: "It's difficult to judge what makes you tired of a thing. Sometimes the eye gets so accustomed that if you don't have a change, you're bored. It's the same way with fashion. And that, I suppose, is what style is all about."

ON HIS BEDROOM: "It's my favorite room in the house," says Blass, who thinks a bedroom needs a really comfortable bed with lots of pillows, an excellent reading lamp, and phone, magazines, and books close at hand. "I have a marvelous collection of old fashion magazines and am apt to work in bed with them propped up around me." When he dines alone "I'm apt to have a tray in here at the desk," but his favorite use of the room is for entertaining. "The fire goes all the time, and people come in for a drink before dinner and pile up on the bed to talk after dinner. It's the focal point of the apartment."

ON HIS DRESSING AREA: "Believe me, it's not the *American Gigolo* scene, although I wish it were." But it is an enviable spot. Behind one set of doors, a counter top and drawers show off their contents; behind another set: shirts (mostly silk), ties, belts, sweaters, and shoes. "How long has it been since you've seen a pair of well-polished shoes?" asks Blass, who feels a good shine is a must.

1980

reciprocated. He remains the most sought-after escort of society's grandes dames. Asked to account for his popularity, Blass offers jovially, "Maybe it's because I have two dinner jackets."

He does say he possesses a prodigious, and genuine, interest in and curiosity about people, and adds, appropriately enough, that the only career other than designer he could have envisioned for himself is that of a diplomat.

Also key to the Blass charm is an impeccable code of manners. "I think good manners are incredibly important," says Blass. Accordingly, Blass

1982

says the men who influenced him most in his early life were Serge Obolensky and Reed Vreeland—"two men who stood out because they always made one feel very welcome, interested in what one was doing."

While close friends of Blass are quick to praise his gentlemanly deportment, dry wit, and matinee-idol good looks, they say the most profound source of his appeal lies in something more substantial—a deep kindliness, compassion, and instinctive generosity with people.

Says fellow designer and close friend Oscar de la Renta, "In a profession where we all have such egos, I think he's fabulously unselfish. I think for him friendship comes before anything."

"I've never known anyone who wasn't rooting for him," agrees designer Mollie Parnis. "You hear about other designers, 'Oh, he walks over dead bodies.' I've never heard that said about Bill."

"He's appreciating life more than he ever did," observes another friend. "He looks it. When I see him, I see a happy man. There's a serenity about him now." Blass is inclined to agree with this last judgment. "I suppose I was very definitely depressed about ten years ago—it has to do with one's personal life, with one's assessment of oneself. But the last four or five years I've been fairly content."

His greatest pleasures come in being with small groups of friends—preferably people he's known a long time—reading as many as five books a week, collecting the dizzyingly eclectic range of prints, antiques, and bibelots that fill his apartment, and, most important, spending time in his eighteenth-century house in New Preston, Connecticut, with his beloved golden retrievers, Kate and Brutus.

"It's the tranquility, the quiet time

1986

1983

in my life. When I'm outside reading, and the dogs are in the pool, it gives me a sense of peace. It's the necessary balance if one sees a lot of people. I'm in bed at nine and up at six."

If there are bêtes noires lurking in the corners of Blass's life, he takes pains to conceal them, and friends of Blass say they never see him depressed or moody. "I find blowing up, losing your temper, showing you're upset is a part of oneself that shouldn't be publicly exposed. If one is bothered, one should walk around one's apartment at three in the morning. That's partly the army—it taught me discipline, also to accept the situation I was in and make the best of it."

On the subject of his future, Blass says, "I think it's unlikely I'd retire; I don't think that's ever the answer. Here again, I don't try to predict—either the pleasures or the disappointments."

—NEW YORK, 1982

1982

1986   1984

1986

1987

1986

1984

1984

THE BLASS STYLE

I f you think you've arrived at a life-style," says Bill Blass, "you haven't got one. It's too pat, too set. And style isn't a set thing." Blass may like "a little flexibility, for God's sake," but with his regimen, it's decidedly hard to come by.

During the week, Blass is up at 7 A.M., showers, shaves, and gets back into bed to read the *New York Times* and eat the breakfast—grapefruit juice, an English muffin, and coffee—that his housekeeper has brought in. He's at the office by 9 and breaks up the "hectic day" by lunching uptown about three times a week.

If Blass doesn't have a 5:30 meeting uptown with his business manager, he tries to walk the two miles home from Seventh Avenue "as often as possible." Or, if he's going out that night, he'll have a limousine pick him up at the office and keep the car for evening.

When Blass arrives at his seven-room penthouse, he pours some Finlandia vodka to sip in a hot tub, which is followed by a cold shower. Wrapped in a cashmere robe in winter, or a cotton wrapper in summer, he lounges on his bed to read his mail and make personal calls, but not to nap.

"My top priority when I'm home is my personal comfort. I work hard, so I want the least amount of problems once I get here." A housekeeper deals with the weekday household hassles—"cleaning, looking after my clothes, preparing breakfast."

What also adds to that "creature comfort" feeling in winter for Blass are the working fireplaces in the living room and bedroom, which are always set so he just has to light them. In summer Blass favors the terrace garden—dotted with weeping willows, flowering crab trees, and Japanese maples—that sweeps around the entire apartment. In warm weather he keeps all of the doors and windows leading out open "so it brings the outside in, and it's like being in the country."

For Blass, "taste must always evolve, not change. You edit, remove, and replace with better things as you can afford them. You don't change your basic concept but improve the things within that concept."

His living room, for example, has seen several incarnations, all under the direction of Mac II. "The living room has changed character because there are more things in it now. I can't help but collect. It's one of the things that makes traveling exciting."

Blass says he used to have people in "at least once a week," but because he has been "preoccupied with trips and my country house," it's been curtailed.

"Entertainment takes thought, a lot of anticipation, and it ain't that much

The 1965 version of Blass's living room

different from running a business. It's an awful lot of involvement if you work, and I don't have a wife." What he has instead is a free-lance cook who also does Blass's dinner-party food shopping.

A typical Blass guest list might include Diana Vreeland, Slim Keith, and Fred Hughes. "If the Lazars [Swifty and Mary] are coming, then it's a different cast. I certainly don't mind an odd number of people, such as five or seven. That way, if someone from out of town arrives unexpectedly, we can just extend the table. I encourage fellas not to wear ties, and a gal can wear anything."

A Blass dinner is likely to start with "a light and cold first course" such as Maryland crabmeat vinaigrette or celery rémoulade, followed by a "simple but substantial main course." Menus are definitely hearty: boiled beef with fresh horseradish, leeks, carrots, and turnips; shepherd's pie, in which fish is sometimes substituted for meat; or broiled lamb cutlets accompanied by a purée of Brussels sprouts and a basket of buttered and seasoned potato-skin shells. He likes light desserts of fruit, such as oranges in wine, along with homemade cookies. His favorite red wine is a 1971 Château Simard St.-Emilion, but he always keeps "a Muscadet on hand because lots of people start with white wine and stick with it through dinner."

For Blass, "getting time under control would be the ultimate luxury. I'm interested in lots of things, but I can't take anything on without getting involved in it. I have other priorities, so entertaining is minimal. I'm not desperate to see people, baby."

BB on How a Man Should Dress

If anyone can afford to be casual about his personal style, it would surely be Bill Blass. Whether in a gray flannel suit or gabardine trousers with a Shetland sweater tied around his shoulders, Blass presents a formidable picture of style.

What's most important about the way a man dresses, says Blass, is that "one dresses for his way of life." He adds that, regardless of lifestyle, "anyone is not well dressed if too coordinated, too thought out or well matched." It's that casual—not messy—look, accomplished with a certain amount of individual style, and the right clothes, that makes the well-dressed man. How to dress with Blass style?

SUITS: No longer mandatory in many instances, he says, but lists three that cover all necessities: a gray flannel, a navy serge, and a chalk stripe.

SHIRTS: "You shouldn't experiment with color but find the best one for you and stick with it. I've been wearing an ivory color for years. White is very hard to wear."

SPORTSWEAR: "Sort of an update of the Ivy League look—subtle woven checks, tattersalls, sweaters, sports jackets. The look of quality—old money."

AT NIGHT: Blass likes a "worn" evening look. "Men are usually better dressed at night than women, because they wear their dinner jacket like an old sports coat—they feel relaxed in it. It's unfortunate that the ruffled shirt ever caught on for evening."

SHOES: "There's no ironbound rule. It's really to do with the whim. One usually wears black shoes with dark suits. The key is keeping them simple—not to have too many, as with shirts. It's easier for travel, et cetera."

HANDKERCHIEFS: "Use one if it fits the look. Sometimes I like a foulard, just shoved in, never pointed."

CUFFS: "Half an inch to three-quarters should show at the most."

TROUSER LENGTH: "You should never see the top of the shoe."

VESTS: "They should be worn, if it's not too hot, for a dressed-up look, to complete a suit, giving it a more important appearance; for an interesting contrast, with a sports jacket and a pair of pants instead of a suit. For evening I like a grosgrain vest with a dinner jacket. Unbuttoning the last button depends on comfort."

ACCESSORIES: "Only those you actually use—a watch and a wedding ring if it means something."

And what are the pitfalls of men's dressing? "Men in America tend to be overweight and make matters worse by wearing clothes that are too big for them—the Zero Mostel look—or too small—the Oliver Hardy look. Ill-fitting clothes are one of the biggest problems." Also bad: "Dressing youthfully when you're past the first flush of youth and being sheepish by dressing like everyone else. The problem is, only a handful of men have the security to care what they look like."

Willy with "Sal"...

..."Kit"...

..."Judums"...

..."Miss"...

..."Luigi"...

Heavenly Harem: Willy and His Gals

Bill Blass is all things to all women. Or at least to the eight loyal ladies who make up his all-American harem and on whom Master Willy has bestowed silly, though coveted, nicknames.

Pat ("Patter") Buckley finds him "cozy," while Missy ("Miss") Bancroft says Blass "reeks of masculinity." To Judy ("Judums") Peabody, he is "the epitome of style and grace," but Katherine ("Kit") Liberman sees Blass as a "vulnerable, corn-fed boy." Geraldine ("Gerald") Stutz likes it best when Blass "is barking bossy orders." Nancy ("Nan") Kissinger claims he personifies the eternal "conflict between intelligence and imagination," and Louise ("Luigi") Melhado suggests he is "one of the few people with soul." Sally ("Sal") Debenham of San Francisco is fond of "that wicked sense of humor that

just laps around your ankles."

It's all a bit cutesy, perhaps, but that's how it should be. Harems, at least in New York, aren't meant to be serious affairs. There are occasional complications, of course. One of Blass's closest friends, and a harem member of good standing, recently confided, "I would have married Bill anytime he asked me, but he never did." Another once reportedly clawed his face when Blass resisted her overtures.

But by and large the Blass harem is a harem of friendship and long-standing affection. "Oscar [de la Renta] is at his most appealing when he's being a flirt and a tease," says Stutz. "Bill is at his most appealing when he's being the bossy, loving big brother." In addition to heaps of fraternal advice, the ladies of the Blass harem get a sought-after escort, the guidance of one of New York's premier taste makers, and, as Kit Liber-

man puts it, "years of chuckles." The master receives many of the same rewards, as well as a bird's-eye view of powerful women at work. "Women dominate this town, this country," notes Blass. "It's all done quietly and subtly, and it's that quiet domination I find fascinating."

When it comes to women, Blass claims to be a traditionalist: Though he likes what he calls "the sharp ones," he is also clearly enamored of "the feminine types." "I can't understand why in the world in the 1980s any woman would consider being 'feminine' an unattractive feature," Blass says. "Men certainly don't find it an insult to be considered masculine."

Blass defines "feminine" as "the opposite of being a fella," and cautions that it has nothing to do "with wearing dresses slit down to your navel." A feminine woman, according to Blass, "abounds in charm," has a good sense of humor, dresses well, looks "appealing," and always maintains an aura of mystery. "I think it's a mistake to know absolutely everything about everybody," suggests Blass. "The Feminine Mystique—and I don't mean Betty Friedan's book—is a powerful weapon."

The litmus test, at least for Blass, occurs over dinner, a meal Social Bill rarely takes alone. He prefers "the gals that work at it," adding, "I know it sounds chauvinistic, but the clever woman is the woman who makes men feel important. That's an indication, I suppose, that many men feel less important these days and we depend on women to give us the illusion, if only for an evening, that we are something we might not be."

The other Blass essential is humor. "I think the thing that makes Pat Buckley a total delight is her ability to laugh,

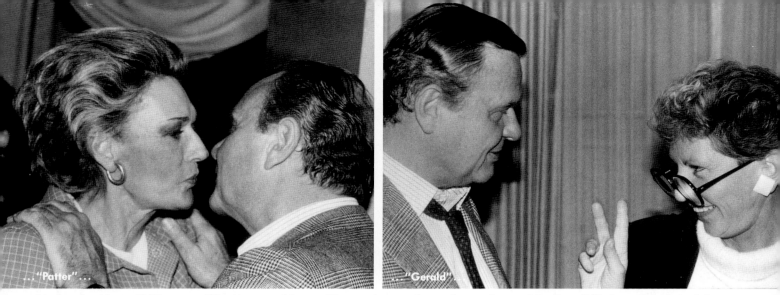

..."Patter"...

..."Gerald"...

and to laugh at herself," he says. "Just to be funny for the sake of giggling is a bore."

Not coincidentally, Buckley admires the same quality in Blass. "He has that all-important asset, a well-developed sense of the ridiculous," she says. "I can be at a dinner with Bill and whisper three words to him and he gets my meaning immediately. We're both covered in gales of laughter and nobody else can figure out what these two fools are carrying on about."

Says Nancy Kissinger, "There are many people in New York you can talk with at a party and it's all laughs and giggles. But you know that as soon as you leave they're going to say something malicious about you. Bill isn't like that. He is totally honorable."

By all accounts, it's not easy to win Blass's friendship ("It takes a long, long time," notes Stutz), and he himself defines his approach to new people as "casual."

"If my manner seems somewhat breezy on first impression that's because I think that's the best way to arrive at somebody, to observe their personality. If a friendship develops in the course of an evening, or during a lunch, fine. If not, that's fine too."

Once captured, however, Blass is captured wholeheartedly. Bancroft has made him the godfather of her three children, and says, "He doesn't go away without calling to say where he is and when he's coming back."

"He's the world's best person to talk to," says Peabody. "The extraordinary thing about Bill is he's nonjudgmental. You can do the worst things and he doesn't put you down. He's also extremely thoughtful. He doesn't just listen to you over lunch and forget your

problems. He ponders and worries and calls you back a dozen times."

Though Blass admits that "from time to time I have difficulty keeping a secret," his ladies value him for his discretion. "He'll never repeat anything," insists Kissinger.

"Women tend to hurl themselves at Bill," suggests one of his harem. "Most of us have tried it once or twice. He's sexy and charming and better-looking than most husbands. You can't blame us for trying."

According to Bancroft, Blass "has all those superb masculine qualities—protection, strength, caring, gentleness, and intelligence." But, as these women, and Blass, make clear, he isn't "one of the boys" they can dish with about maids and makeup. "God, the last thing I

would talk to Bill about is hair and dresses," notes Bancroft. "I might ask him a question about how I look, and he'll give me a straight answer, whether I like it or not, but that's as far as it goes."

"I don't think of myself as a substitute husband, either," adds Blass. "When you have that rare thing called friendship with a woman it's based on many mutual interests—other people, books, theater, music, paintings, furniture, those things that make one's life important."

Blass denies that he has any particular knack for dealing with women. "I treat them the same way I would treat a man," he says. "After all, men and women are searching for the same thing from each other. We all want companionship, humor, a sense of belonging to another person. I think the most appealing thing about any relationship is that sense of belonging."

Blass estimates that three of his five closest friends are women, and though these friendships are on what he calls "an intellectual level," there is, he ad-

...and "Nan"

Bill Blass clothes bring an attention-getting snap to the woman who dresses to wound, if not to kill. At their best, they have the dizzying dryness of a vodka martini.

1985

mits, an inevitable "sexual overtone. Between men and women there's always a sexual attraction on the part of one or the other. It's always lying there below the surface, if it doesn't actually explode."

Much to his discomfort, there are frequent explosions. "Women tend to hurl themselves at Bill," suggests one of the harem. "Most of us have tried it once or twice. He's sexy and charming and better-looking than most husbands. You can't blame us for trying."

Blass is invariably polite, if somewhat skittish, when one of the ladies puts the moves on him. One brash playgirl, not a member of the harem, recalls a seduction scene several years ago at a boozy Manhattan party. "There we were kissing madly," she claims. "It was midnight and we were in a discreet corner and I thought, 'Well, I've got him—finally.' In the middle of everything, he whispers, 'Let me up for a second, I have to go to the men's room.' He went, and I didn't see him again for three years."

All of the harem members are exceedingly proud of Blass's good looks. "I think he looks like [football star] Terry Bradshaw's older brother," says Liberman. "Every time I catch him sucking in those cheeks trying to be like Rex Harrison, I tell him, 'Stop that, Bill. Just be yourself.'" "I've known a lot of men in my time," adds Bancroft, "and Bill is one of the most attractive. He is handsome, clean, and polished."

Not all is sweetness and light, of course. Blass, says the harem, can be difficult, grumpy (especially when he's tired), and, on occasion, even jealous. And he can also be a terrible flirt. "The ladies in San Francisco go crazy over him when he comes," notes Debenham. "The competition to have him to lunch or dinner is fierce."

But these minor failings are more than compensated by Blass's legendary panache. "He possesses true elegance, none of that la-di-da stuff," declares Bancroft. "I've never known Bill to buy a piece of furniture that wasn't pleasing or cook a meal that wasn't delicious or hang a painting that wasn't impeccable."

But all of this only hints at Blass's success, only partially explains why he is the master of the great American harem. The final answer, according to Stutz, is glaringly simple. "We're crazy about him because he's crazy about us," she says. "Willy is a man who loves women."   —NEW YORK, 1984

BILL BLASS 219

ALL-AMERICAN BLASS

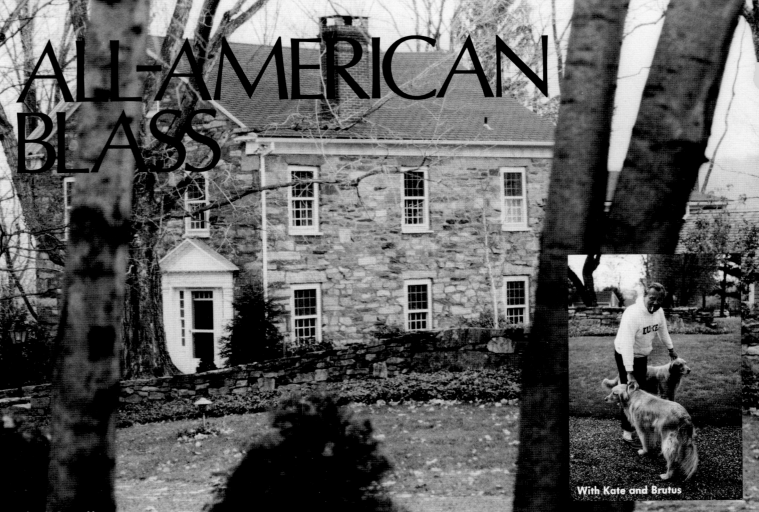

Blass's Stone House

With Kate and Brutus

Stone House, built as a tavern in the eighteenth century, has known several illustrious visitors: George Washington, the Marquis de La-Fayette, and now Bill Blass. "The house was not at all what I was looking for," says Blass, who looked for two years before he bought the place in 1976. "I had in mind that I wanted a huge, rambling, remote house. Instead, I found an old tavern right on what used to be the town square, probably built between 1770 and 1780. I liked the fact that it has a certain dignity, a certain style."

Blass says the real reason he bought the house was the property. It includes twenty-two acres of wooded land and a wonderfully New England setting: twisting road, enormous maples, and, across the road, sturdy Hill Church. "Only open two months a year, thank God."

Blass notes that while George Washington never slept in the tavern, he did meet there with some French generals, and Blass points out that the parlor was once ladies' and gents' waiting rooms. "That's why it has two fireplaces," he says, adding, "I furnished it rather sparsely, which I think suits the style of this house."

Upstairs are the master bedroom and the two guest rooms. Blass notes, "Don't forget that this was a tavern, not an inn. Originally, there were no bedrooms at all." There are, however, plenty of fireplaces—seven in all.

The kitchen, he says, is his favorite room, "a room where I entertain. I use the kitchen for dining, and I guess the only thing in the room that isn't English or American is a tall cupboard from an Italian barracks. It's about sixteenth-century and it once held flags and standards, but the simplicity of it seems to fit so well in this Early American house." There is a charming eclectic mix of objects in it—a favorite pink dogwood platter, his collection of Mocha ware, an Austrian mirror.

The dining room is cozy, with an attractive, all-purpose fireplace that probably got quite a workout during the house's early life. "I've seated ten at a round catering table I usually keep stored," says Blass, but he prefers small dinner groups of six, who can gather at the oval-shaped table that is the normal centerpiece of the room. Blass creates different moods for this basically neutral environment with an unending supply of table coverings—"mostly Bill Blass."

What Blass likes in the country is "quite American," from his Lee jeans to the food from his kitchen. "For lunch on a chilly day, I might serve cold pasta, homemade baked beans, ham, a wonderful mustard, fruit, and corn muffins." For dessert: American apple pie and Cheddar cheese.

"There's no compulsion to entertain here the way there is in the Hamptons," he says. "Nobody drops in unexpectedly. I have time for the greatest love of my life: to have time alone." There's also time to work in the kitchen producing pasta and meatloaf. Other culinary offerings are left in the capable hands of the housekeeper.

"This is the kind of thing that's easy to prepare for a Friday night," says the

A corner for informal meals

A view to the dining room

A tabletop of little treasures

Fluffy towels
in the guest house

The fruits of antiquing forays

designer about his meatloaf-based dinner that begins with hot cream of artichoke soup and ends with hot apple brown Betty with vanilla ice cream.

Driven from New York on Fridays, Blass gets a head start on his weekend guests, who usually arrive around seven. Readying the meatloaf takes less than twenty minutes, and cooking it an hour. Provisions, from the ground sirloin ("people who tell you the grade of meat for a meatloaf doesn't matter don't know what they're talking about") to the homemade bread, are procured locally.

Friday-night dinners, as all weekend meals, are low-key affairs served by a young woman who lives nearby. They are early nights. "Some people here, especially the theater crowd, stay up until three in the morning. I think that after eleven-thirty you've really said all there is to say."

DESIGNER MEATLOAF

This is one of those recipes that change with the individual cook. There are measured ingredients: three pounds ground sirloin; one egg; two medium-sized onions, chopped; two and a half stalks of celery, chopped; one small can of V-8 juice ("never tomato"). And there are estimated additions: dashes of sea salt and pepper; generous sprinklings of marjoram, thyme, and tarragon; a few hearty shakes from a can of bread crumbs, and from a bottle of Worcestershire sauce.

Blass combines all these ingredients and mixes them well with his hands and then forms the loaf, which serves five or six. The loaf is lavishly top-coated with Heinz chili sauce and then with six strips of bacon. It's put in a preheated 350-degree oven for an hour. Blass also recommends the mixture, uncooked, for steak tartare.

Blass's gravy is another fickle creation, with Franco American beef gravy as its base. He chops about a dozen mushrooms, sautés them in butter, adds a can of the beef gravy, and pours in enough red wine to give a generous taste. The final ingredient is pan drippings from the meatloaf dish.

The guest house's rear deck

The guest house living room

Blass's guesthouse, at the end of a stone walk and down the hill from the main house, offers a luxurious mix of rustic charm and sophisticated amenities: stacks of fluffy towels in the bathroom, a rear deck with a view of the meadow, and a capacious living area with a giant fireplace. "I'm a stickler," says Blass, who provides guests with everything from homemade cookies to raincoats and stocks the fridge in the tiny, enclosed kitchen with wine.

The host maintains that the best guests are the ones who can take care of themselves. "Billy Rayner does watercolors here. I subscribe to every magazine there is and keep the place full of books." Blass himself likes "to walk and putter around a lot in jeans and boots," and there is poolside activity in the summer and antique outings in the fall. "My greatest pleasure is searching for objects and antiques, but I'm not dead serious about it. I find it a wonderful diversion."

This is definitely a place where a car is a necessity. But despite promptings from friends (Gerry Stutz gave him driving lessons one Christmas), Blass remains without a license and sees no pressing need to change his status. "I have a car and a friend will drive me, or guests will have a car we can use." Social outings are kept to a minimum distance. "I take a dim view of traveling more than twenty minutes for dinner."

Summing up, Blass says, "What one tries to do here, and I suppose in the rest of one's life, is to simplify. It seems to me that there is too much of everything, too many objects in our life. Simplicity is very, very necessary to me."
—New Preston, CONNECTICUT, 1984

Setting out a picnic

1987

DATE DUE

APR 12			
APR 2 7 1994			

GAYLORD | | | PRINTED IN U.S.A.